PRAISE FOR
Cindy Margolis and *Having a Baby* . . .

"Tackles a delicate issue with courage, wisdom, and generosity. . . . Personal, easy to read, and possessed of a warm, welcome sense of humor, Margolis's book makes an excellent introduction for anyone facing fertility issues, putting a hopeful face on a distressing topic, providing much-needed support, and pointing the way forward."

—*Publishers Weekly*

"I'm so proud of Cindy's contribution to millions of parents-to-be."

—Vicki Iovine,
author of *The Girlfriends' Guide to Pregnancy*

"We could not have been more pleased when Cindy Margolis chose to work with RESOLVE to help create greater awareness, information, and support for the thousands of women and men struggling with infertility. Cindy is a young, dynamic, vibrant woman, and an international celebrity, who is passionate and articulate about the challenges of infertility. She and her husband, Guy, know firsthand the emotional and physical challenges of infertility, as well as the true joy of having a baby."

—Joseph C. Isaacs, CAE,
President and CEO of RESOLVE:
The National Infertility Association

Having a Baby...

When the Old-Fashioned
Way Isn't Working

Hope and Help for
Everyone Facing Infertility

Cindy Margolis

with Kathy Kanable

Snunit Ben-Ozer, M.D., Medical Adviser

A PERIGEE BOOK

A PERIGEE BOOK
Published by the Penguin Group
Penguin Group (USA) Inc.
375 Hudson Street, New York, New York 10014, USA

Penguin Group (Canada), 90 Eglinton Avenue East, Suite 700, Toronto, Ontario M4P 2Y3, Canada (a division of Pearson Penguin Canada Inc.) • Penguin Books Ltd., 80 Strand, London WC2R 0RL, England • Penguin Group Ireland, 25 St. Stephen's Green, Dublin 2, Ireland (a division of Penguin Books Ltd.) • Penguin Group (Australia), 250 Camberwell Road, Camberwell, Victoria 3124, Australia (a division of Pearson Australia Group Pty. Ltd.) • Penguin Books India Pvt. Ltd., 11 Community Centre, Panchsheel Park, New Delhi—110 017, India • Penguin Group (NZ), 67 Apollo Drive, Rosedale, North Shore 0632, New Zealand (a division of Pearson New Zealand Ltd.) • Penguin Books (South Africa) (Pty.) Ltd., 24 Sturdee Avenue, Rosebank, Johannesburg 2196, South Africa

Penguin Books Ltd., Registered Offices: 80 Strand, London WC2R 0RL, England

While the author has made every effort to provide accurate telephone numbers and Internet addresses at the time of publication, neither the publisher nor the author assumes any responsibility for errors, or for changes that occur after publication. Further, the publisher does not have any control over and does not assume any responsibility for author or third-party websites or their content.

PRINTING HISTORY
Perigee hardcover edition / January 2008
Perigee trade paperback edition / January 2009

Perigee trade paperback ISBN: 978-0-399-53479-9

The Library of Congress has cataloged the Perigee hardcover edition as follows:

Margolis, Cindy.
  Having a baby—when the old-fashioned way isn't working: hope and help for everyone facing infertility/Cindy Margolis, with Kathy Kanable; medical adviser, Snunit Ben-Ozer.—1st ed.
    p. cm.
  ISBN 978-0-399-53385-3
    1. Margolis, Cindy. 2. Infertility, Female—Patients—United States—Biography. 3. Fertilization in vitro, Human—United States—Popular works. 4. Human reproductive technology—United States—Popular works. I. Kanable, Kathy. II. Ben-Ozer, Snunit. III. Title.
  RG201.M37 2008
  362.198'1780092—dc22
  [B]   2007028014

PRINTED IN THE UNITED STATES OF AMERICA

10 9 8 7 6 5 4 3 2 1

PUBLISHER'S NOTE: Neither the publisher nor the author is engaged in rendering professional advice or services to the individual reader. The ideas, procedures, and suggestions contained in this book are not intended as a substitute for consulting with your physician. All matters regarding your health require medical supervision. Neither the author nor the publisher shall be liable or responsible for any loss or damage allegedly arising from any information or suggestion in this book.

CONTENTS

PART 1
Get Thee to a Specialist

PART 2

Other Options for Growing a Family: Surrogacy, Gestational Surrogacy, Third-Party Donors, and Adoption

PART 3

Where Do You Go from Here?

ACKNOWLEDGMENTS

This book has been in my heart for a long time. From our first failed attempt at IVF through the glorious births of our three children, Nicholas, Sierra, and Sabrina. It didn't come easy, that's for sure. Many people and things had to line up in just the right order to make it happen. But here it is—another dream come true for me. And for this, there are so many I need to thank.

The wonderful men and women who came to my website as fans and left as friends—I love you the most! You have opened your hearts and shared your lives with me in ways that only real friends could do. I have learned much from you about life, inner strength, and the pursuit of personal happiness. Thank you for sharing so much of yourselves with me. And to those whose stories also appear in this book, thanks for sharing yourselves with our infertility community as well.

To my husband, Guy . . . yesterday, today, and forever . . . I love you for so many reasons. Your strength and courage that we all count on. The way you love and take care of your family. You are the finest of husbands, the greatest of fathers. And to our beautiful and precious children, Nicholas, Sierra, and Sabrina, who fill our lives with such happiness and the magic of true love every day. You are the reason this book needed to be written.

To the team of women who made this book happen—Marian Lizzi, my publisher at Perigee Books; Laurie Bernstein, my publishing agent; Caroline Pincus, the book midwife; Dr. Snunit Ben-Ozer, M.D., my doctor and medical adviser for this book; and mostly Kathy Kanable, my beloved co-author and best friend. Look what we have done! I'm so proud of all of you and so grateful to have such beautiful and talented women in my life. You have each given me blessings beyond words and proved that together we can do anything!

To Neil Cirucci, my manager, the one person in the world who takes more abuse from me than everyone else combined. He is my sounding board, my ideal man, the guy who keeps my schedule straight and the one who also messes it up! He's a marketing genius, and I thank my lucky stars every day that I have been blessed with his partnership and his friendship for all these years.

To my mother, Karyn, who raised me by herself and made me the woman I am today. She taught me how to work for what I want and give it everything I've got. How to learn from each new experience. How to be honest and real. How to care about people as much as I can. You are my role model. I love you for being a wonderful mother to me and an incredible grandmother to my children.

To Cory, my brother, my friend, whenever I need someone to talk to or just someone to listen. Thanks for always being there for me in ways that no one else ever could. I love you very much.

To Shannon, our surrogate mother, our angel. Thank you

from the bottom of our hearts for giving us the most precious gifts anyone could ever give—the gift of our twin girls, the gift of life.

And finally, to all the couples out there who, like Guy and me, just could not get pregnant the *old-fashioned way*—this book is especially for you. As you carve your own path along the rocky terrain of infertility, remember you are not alone. *Your baby dreams can come true!*

FOREWORD

I often hear the surprise, pain, frustration, anger, self-doubt, and fear of my patients and their partners as I mold the pieces of the medical puzzle into a fertility plan. My heart aches as I relate to my patients on many levels: fertility specialist, woman who delayed childbearing and made provisions for Plan B, woman who found Mr. Right late and had difficulty conceiving.

Great strides have been made in the miraculous field of reproductive endocrinology and infertility (REI) since 1973, the year the first in vitro fertilization baby, Louise Brown, was born in England. Thankfully, these days most patients can achieve their goal of becoming parents, but the journey is sometimes arduous. Patients must navigate through an alphabet soup of medical choices—CC, COH, IVF, PGD, ICSI, AH, GIFT, ZIFT, FET, to name just a few common ones. They need to brace their relationship from an emotional roller coaster fueled by raging hormones and be prepared to jump over financial hurdles. They must silently endure social stigma, well-meaning yet painful advice, and invitations to baby showers and kids' birthday parties from friends and relatives, and try to feign a normal life.

Infertility is nonbiased. It strikes about one in six couples across all reproductive ages, socioeconomic and racial backgrounds, and sexual orientations.

When I first met Cindy Margolis, she, like my other patients, was distraught and frustrated by her situation. "Why me? What have I done, or not done, that I am now suffering this plight?" Of course, I explained to her, as I do to all my patients, that infertility is a medical issue and often has little to do with what you did or didn't do. At first, Cindy and her husband, Guy, like many other couples, felt alone and isolated in their frustration. But as they learned more about the fertility process, its trials and tribulations, Cindy's light began to shine through. Through her tears and suffering, Cindy began to understand not only the medical issues but also the enormity of the additional hardships caused by the infertility shroud of secrecy. Frustrated by the lack of first-person infertility literature and information sharing, she became fiercely determined to help others by breaking the silence.

Even while Cindy was a patient, we spoke about the importance of disseminating the truth about the successes and limitations of medical technology. I have long felt that it is my responsibility, passion, and calling to educate laypeople and physicians (obstetrician/gynecologists, family practitioners, and internists) about fertility as well as to educate and warn young, unsuspecting women and couples about the perils of delaying childbearing and of insurance options such as embryo freezing and sometimes egg freezing. Good information empowers women and couples to make wiser and more informed decisions and helps remove the social stigma and secrecy surrounding infertility.

I believe that having children ought to be an inalienable right for all who can provide a warm, stable, loving home. Unfortunately, for many that right is fraught with hardship. For those women and couples, this book is a guide and support.

I am very excited that Cindy Margolis has written this book and am honored that she asked for my help. It is my hope that all of you who are currently experiencing infertility will find in its pages not only useful, empowering information and the courage to pursue your dream of having a baby but also the comfort of knowing you are not alone.

A few more words in closing: Not all fertility specialists are created equal. Please seek out the very best clinic available to you. Work with someone who listens to your questions and gives you information you can understand, someone who will educate you sufficiently so that you can make the decisions that are right for *you*. You should never feel pressured to undertake a procedure unless and until you are ready.

Even if you have to travel some distance for the care, try to find someone who will support you individually and as a couple through the emotional and physical challenges of treatment, someone who is informed about the latest advances in medical care and can help you maximize your chances of success. These are not unreasonable expectations. They are what you deserve.

I wish you much success.

Snunit Ben-Ozer, M.D.
Reproductive Endocrinology and Infertility
Founder, Tree of Life Center
Associate Clinical Professor
University of California Los Angeles

Welcome to the Reproductively Challenged Club

Do not pass go. Do not collect baby!

I am in the ladies' room of the Beverly Hills Hotel for what must be the fifteenth time tonight—the fifth time in just the past hour. Every few minutes, it seems, I'm checking to see if I'm getting my period. I must be going nuts. No, I must be nuts already, I'm just the only person who doesn't know it yet. I'm sure our dinner partners know it! The look on their faces when I excused myself this time pretty much cinches the fact that my husband, Guy, and I won't be on their A list for any future events.

I am accustomed to being in the spotlight. After all, I'm the Most Downloaded Woman on the Internet. And in a career that spans over twenty years, I've been a supermodel, an actress, an author, and a spokesperson for numerous products and companies. I have been on television in a number of capacities and on the cover of hundreds of magazines in the United States and abroad. But that night and for so many nights before and after I was just one more woman trying—desperately—to have a child. Every year, approximately 10.3 million women and couples try to conceive. We go on an incredibly complicated, emotional journey often without anyone but our partner knowing about it. And that isolation, in itself, can stress you out like nothing else.

This book tells my story—the story of my years of struggle to accomplish the one thing that seemed to come so naturally to everyone else. Or at least that's what I thought when my infertility nightmare first began. Since that time, however, my husband, Guy, and I have learned that we are not alone, that couples all around us are struggling in the same and in many different ways. One of the saddest threads running through all our stories is that there is so little useful information, so few maps, available to any of us traveling down this very rocky road. We didn't have each other to talk to, to swap stories with, to share tips and ideas, and to comfort. Because the issue of infertility is stored on the highest shelf of a very deep closet.

I'm here to change that. This book is an effort to bring infertility out into the open where we can deal with it together. So passionate am I that other couples need a little bit smoother road, a little less complicated information, and a whole lot more support that everything else must now move to the back of the bus for me. As one of the few celebrity pioneers of the Internet, I'm used to taking the road less traveled. Or even the one others will not go down. When RESOLVE: The National Infertility Association first approached me about being their first official celebrity spokesperson, some thought it would be a great risk to my career. "People aren't talking about this stuff, Cindy," they said. "Celebrities aren't talking about it. You will be tagged, labeled, and possibly worse." How could that be? How could something so important, something so a part of who we are as human beings, be such a secret, such a risk?

Falling in love, having a baby, and starting a family are dreams most of us take for granted. We just figure that when the time is right, these things will happen for us, exactly when we want them to, and we will go on to live happily ever after. Finding out that our baby dreams are not so easily fulfilled is first devastating, then almost crippling—to the point that many of us want to give up completely. I know that's what happened to me. I thought I had been so wronged. Why couldn't I have a child? I thought that I was being punished—by whom and for what I did not know. I thought I was not a whole woman and a host of other unhealthy thoughts that would send me to my bed for days on end. Of course, I know now that none of this was my fault.

From one of the darkest corners of my life, however, finally came some of the brightest light. After three years of trying to conceive, first alone and then with a lot of high-tech help, my husband and I did begin our family. That sense of hope and possibility, that *light*, is what I want to share with all of you. Because the truth is, if you want to have a family (and you are reasonably sane and solvent), you will. Somehow, some way, you will. It's so important to remember that.

Finding out you can't have a baby the "old-fashioned way" can be such a huge blow. Bewildering, frightening, depressing, and did I mention stressful? After you read this book, infertility—the Big Secret—will be a secret no more. Not only will you have a

sense of belonging to the large community of us out here struggling to make babies but you will also have our support. You'll
have a better sense of what your options are and how best to
prepare yourself emotionally for the road ahead. For some of
you, it will be a long road; others will be lucky enough to (or
make certain choices that will) shorten it by months or years.
But you *will* make your baby dreams come true.

It's funny, all this secrecy about the Big I. In 2006, when I
started this book, there were more than 9 million women using
infertility services, 9 million *other women besides me* desperately
trying to have a child. I found it hard to believe then that there
were that many people (in the United States alone) with hearts
that ached as badly as ours did. How could that be? Wouldn't
we have heard about it on the six o'clock news or read about
pain of such magnitude in some newspaper or magazine somewhere?

But I soon found out that number was only the tip of the ice-
berg. There are many couples every day who are just learning that
they must face the heartbreak of infertility. They're just starting
on the road that we've been down. So many people who need to
learn from what some of us have already been through. As women
continue to postpone the age at which they marry and start families, the number of infertile couples will continue to rise. How can
it not? As more women begin trying to conceive with the help of
assisted reproductive therapies (ARTs), the need for additional resources also rises, as does the need for the outside world (including
legislatures and insurance companies) to become more enlight-
ened and educated about the difficulties encountered and the resources and support that are desperately needed. These are the

facts, people. We can help each other. But that's only a start. We need a village to remove the stigma.

Living in Los Angeles, I know so many women celebrities who have absolutely no qualms about going on TV to show off a great boob job or to sing the praises of their recent Botox injections or to share an amazing array of other medically intimate details of their lives. But when was the last time you heard a famous woman talk openly about not being able to get pregnant? Can't remember? That's because it isn't spoken aloud. Not even among ourselves, woman to woman or couple to couple. Fear and shame seem to win every time. I aim to change that, too. There are many reasons women don't conceive easily, but *none of them, and I repeat, none of them* is cause for shame.

I have to tell you, in the beginning, I too was ashamed and embarrassed that I couldn't conceive our child the old-fashioned way. So much so, that I almost blew a very important opportunity in my career. I was being interviewed about who my idols were, who I looked up to, and who my role model was. I told the interviewer the story of how I had always loved and looked up to Michelle Pfeiffer. To me, she was the epitome of class and beauty and so very talented as well. Apparently, both Michelle and her husband, David E. Kelley (one of Hollywood's biggest and most successful television producers), were watching the night the interview aired and called to ask me to play myself on one of his top-rated prime-time shows.

Can you imagine? A chance to play *me* on a David E. Kelley show? I was thrilled! For about ten seconds! Because then it hit me. There was going to be a huge bump in this road. The scene called for me to wear a bikini and I was smack dab in the middle of my first round of in vitro fertilization (IVF) medications. Now remember, this was back before people spoke of such things, so I didn't feel like I could tell him, "Hey, I'm having PMS times a *gazillion* this month. . . . You really may not want to see me in a bikini!" So instead, I begged and pleaded and then begged some more to please let me wear something else. Something that would allow me to wear a corset to suck in that extra 15 pounds and cover up my hormone-ravaged body. But of course the more I pleaded the more determined wardrobe and then even David was that I be seen in the bikini!

"You are Cindy Margolis!" he said. "Your bikini-clad images are known the world over, and by God, that's what I want for this scene." How could I tell him (and the rest of the world) that I wasn't being a diva? I would have happily jumped right into that itsy-bitsy-teeny-weeny yellow polka-dot bikini for a shot at playing myself in any one of David's prime-time shows—some other time. But I'm on drugs, people, nasty drugs! Drugs that make you blow up like a sponge soaking up a pail full of water and will surely leave you with an itsy-bitsy bikini image that isn't what you had in mind.

Eventually, we compromised. I did wear a swimsuit, but thank God, it was a one piece with a sarong around my waist. The show got huge ratings, and I was asked back a few weeks later to play in another episode. *Entertainment Tonight* (*ET*) had also called the show and arranged to interview me after my next appearance. By then I had finished my first IVF cycle and suffered the devastation of our first failure. I don't know why, maybe because it was so soon after our first devastating pregnancy failure and Guy and I were still feeling so very lost and alone, but when *ET* asked about how my first experience work-

ing on the show had gone, I just
let loose and spilled my guts, ad-
mitting to the world not only that
was I on drugs during that time,

Lesson one of the infertility
journey: You are not in control.

ashamed of my body, and so embarrassed that people would
find out that I couldn't get pregnant the same way that "normal"
people did but also that I had almost turned down one of the
most prestigious producers in Hollywood and missed the chance
entirely. Well . . . *ET* went worldwide with my IVF/infertility
story. The floodgates were now open, and I can't say that my
poor husband was all that happy about his sperm being talked
about on *ET* that evening, but the admission eventually led to
this book. And that's a good thing!

Lesson one of the infertility journey: You are not in control.
Try as you might, you cannot will your body to become or stay
pregnant. It just doesn't work that way.

If you, too, are traveling the infertility road, I want you to
know that you're in very good company. If you've had trouble
even saying the words, don't worry. From this point on we're going to say them together. I'm going to provide you with the information you need and direct you to people to talk to; I'm going
to explain the treatment options and tell you about the doctors
and centers in your area that offer the information and services
you need. I'm going to outline for you exactly what questions
you need to ask and when you need to start asking them.

I'm also going to share the stories of a number of other
women and couples just like us who are facing the same strug-
gles and conquering the same obstacles. Their stories are not so
very different from the millions of others unfolding across the
world. The friends and acquaintances who share their stories

here did not end up with the exact same outcomes: Most realized their baby dreams, though often with some alterations. A few gave up their dreams. How far you are willing or able to go to create a family is an intensely personal decision. No one else can make it for you.

However, you can take it from me, if your own experience hasn't convinced you: Having information, resources, and support can make all the difference. If Guy and I had had a book like this when we discovered that the old-fashioned way wasn't working, we would not have had to muddle our way through the world of infertility on our own!

Now I have to warn you. In case you hadn't noticed, I'm not the withholding type. This is going to be a very candid book. If you tend toward the squeamish, get over it! If you're going to have a baby, you'll need to check your hang-ups at the first chapter. Infertility just isn't a pretty picture. It wasn't for us or for anyone else I know. You're going to read about cervical mucus (it's amazing what you can learn about your own reproductive cycle by paying attention to what's happening *down there*), medications that can make you a little crazy, and the possibility of getting daily shots in your butt as well as such juicy topics as who needs to be on top for the best penetration.

You think these things don't matter? Think again. When you're trying to have a baby, everything matters. What you ate for breakfast matters, and what your partner didn't eat matters, too. Hell, what kind of underwear he wears and how often he soaks in a hot bath are important here, too!

I will tell you how you can still have sex with a man who only minutes before made you so angry you thought just touching him would make you vomit. Or how you can make love to the man with whom you've had baby-making sex so often you don't feel like doing it ever again. I will describe what it feels like to feel so sorry for yourself that you can't imagine getting out of bed, and I will also tell you how to overcome it so that you can move on to what's really important in your quest to bear a child.

And I'll keep reminding you that your infertility is *not your fault*.

We'll talk about the medical aspects for sure. Even the practical ones. But we'll also talk about the physical and emotional aspects of this journey—which no one, and I mean *no one*, else is talking about. By the time you're done reading this book, you may know more about me than you do about yourself. But more important, you will also know every little thing about:

- What you need to do

- Who you need to see

- What resources are available to you to help you conceive a child

For when all is said and done, that's all that matters. Of course I can't guarantee you'll get pregnant, much as I might like to. But I can promise you that where there's a will, there *is* most definitely a way. If you want a baby, a baby you will have.

So join me. Say the words with me right now, out loud:

I'm having trouble getting pregnant. I need some help.

Whew! That was hard! But that part's over. Now, let's get moving.

PART 1

Get Thee to a Specialist

CHAPTER 1

Our Story

I want to tell you a little bit about me and Guy.

On September 6, 1998, after meeting him on a blind date and being with him for a year and a half, I married the man of my dreams, restaurateur Guy Starkman. Right away, I knew he would make an amazing father. He was a wonderfully compassionate man, kind, patient, and more tolerant of other people than anyone I had ever met. He was also still a little boy at heart, and I could just imagine him playing with our kids and showing them the world. It was also a wonderful time in our lives—full of family, friends, joy, and promise.

I had also always wanted kids, and we didn't waste any time deciding to try to get pregnant. We wanted to start a family right away and what better way to enjoy your honeymoon than to try, try, try to conceive?

We had two weeks of the most amazing, nonstop sex you could imagine. We made love in the hotel room, on the balcony, in the hallway (Yes! In the middle of the night when we thought no one was looking). We had sex on the beach, sex in the ocean, on a beach chair, in our cabana, in the woods, around the coral reef, while swimming with the dolphins, on a swing, in a tree, behind the swim-up bar, under a moonlit skyline, and in the Jacuzzi as the sun rose each morning. We had romantic sex, hot sex, steamy sex, drunk on our love sex, passionate sex, not-so-passionate sex, sex with fervor. Sex in the bathtub, sex in the pool, and even sex under the snack bar! I swore there was no way I could return home from our favorite hotel in Maui and not be pregnant.

I would have been thrilled to return home with morning sickness. But that was not to be. And the arrival of that disappointing period was only the first jolt in a long line of months of frustration and disappointment to come. In fact I would spend the next several *years* getting our hopes up month after month after month, only to be sadly disappointed when, once again, my period would arrive like clockwork.

By the end of the first year of our marriage, when we were still without happy baby news to share with friends and family, I had become somewhat obsessed with the whole process. I certainly knew we were having *enough* sex and was pretty sure we were having it at all the appropriate times in my cycle. So why was I not being blessed with a child?

As each period came and went, I started having crazy thoughts. I thought I was being punished for my past mistakes. I should never have cheated on my first love with that cute actor who turned out to be a jerk! If I hadn't maybe I would be pregnant now. I became very superstitious and religious. I set up a baby shrine by my bed with a collage of baby pictures; I wrote letters to my unborn baby; I lit fertility candles, saw a psychic and then a healer, and even had my stomach blessed by a priest, a rabbi, and a minister. When all that didn't work, I was convinced it was because God saw through me.

Sure, I had prayed before, my family had always observed and respected all the holidays, but I

> Most causes of infertility are medical and have absolutely nothing to do with what you did or didn't do, what you are or aren't doing. It's not your fault!

wouldn't have exactly been called religious—and had never really appreciated the power of faith. Now I was positive that God saw my intentions as insincere. "I'm being punished again," I thought. "He (or she or the devil or somebody!) doesn't want me to get pregnant." I figured I had somehow given up the right or given away my chance. Something I had done or not done must explain why I was being kicked to the curb. So went the running monologue in my head for more than a year.

No one would have known how awful I felt. To the outside world it probably looked like I had it all. I was a successful businesswoman; I had a handsome and devoted husband and supportive friends and family; millions of fans visited my website each month. My career was in full swing. But inside I was breaking, and my heart hurt all the time. When I wasn't feeling like a big failure, I would convince myself that my husband was minutes away from leaving me for a younger woman who could give him the baby—and family—he (and I) so badly wanted. Did I mention that I had those thoughts *every day*?

Among my friends, we didn't talk about it. It just wasn't discussed, although I've since learned that several of my closest friends traveled this same road. Some before me. All of us alone.

Which is exactly why I *did* start talking about it. And when I did, many would hush me up or worse. I've had big-name celebrities corner me in the bathroom and say, "What are you doing? Are you crazy? You can't talk about this stuff!"

My life was a mess, and the stress only got worse with each negative pregnancy test. Guy wanted to be there for me, but more often than not he felt as helpless and alone as I did. We were together every day, in the same house, at the same dinner table each night, but we were worlds apart in our own personal pain and misery.

Meanwhile, we were having nonstop sex (and trust me, that's just not as much fun as it sounds) and getting nowhere. If I thought I was ovulating, I would call Guy off the basketball court, out of a meeting, away from a family function, and even home early from a business trip. Trust me, I was fast becoming the not-so-popular wife among even our closest circle of friends and business associates. I made Guy promise to never, and I mean *never*, be without his cell phone or without his cell phone on; and if he didn't answer on the very first ring, I would jump all over him for not wanting this baby badly enough, for not trying as hard as he needed to. I even told him once that if he didn't get home within ten minutes and have sex with me, I'd find someone else who would! Which was just a lovely way to start a lovemaking session once he did arrive home, don't you think?

And the months continued to roll by. No little blue or pink dot. Not even a stick to pee on. My periods were as punctual as Swiss trains.

The Dipstick Test

I have to take a little time out here and say a couple of get-real words about getting your period. Every month, as the time for my period would approach, I would participate in an unusual little ritual, something known as "the dipstick test" to those who went before me. But of course I didn't know that then. At the time, I thought it was just yet another crazy behavior unique to moi. It went something like this: Each month, as the date for my period neared, I'd find myself sticking a piece of tissue or toilet paper down my pants to see if it showed blood. I became so good at it that I could actually do the quick check while seated on a crowded airplane, even with the flight attendant standing next to me! I would and could discreetly wipe and view just about anywhere and nobody was the wiser. In the car, the kitchen, a restaurant, on my way to an appearance, even on the set of *Hollywood Squares* as they were taping in front of a live audience!

I know it sounds crazy, but here's the thing. It's actually quite normal and sane. So when you start playing this game yourself don't go off the deep end about it. I only wish I'd had someone to tell me how normal this was. Instead I worried myself sick. I worried that it was a silly thing to do or that someone would notice, but I worried more that each time I withdrew my hand I would see the dreaded red/brown splotch.

And then I turned thirty-five.

We spent my thirty-fifth birthday with friends and family. Guy planned a wonderful dinner, bought me a beautiful necklace, and showered me with a day full of physical and emotional

> **Fertility notably diminishes in our mid-thirties.**

pampering. He could not have been more attentive to me or to the details of my entire day and evening celebration. I have an amazing husband, for sure; but all his efforts did little to ease the pain of realizing that I was yet another year past my prime childbearing years. Oh yeah, thirty-five was a very hard birthday for me. We had been trying to conceive for almost two years already. Despite all the attention, I couldn't help but feel used up and useless.

I excused myself at every opportunity, preferring to spend whatever time I could away from the prying eyes of my husband and family, desperate to hide the torrent of uncontrollable tears that seemed to spontaneously well up inside of me all the time those days. Irrational as it was, I was convinced that my thirty-fifth birthday meant my life was over. I was sure I would never have children in my life. In our life. Ever.

I cried myself to sleep that night, waking up the next day with such swollen eyes that it was hours before I could really even see my own reflection in the mirror. Of course, because God was most definitely not smiling on me, I had a photo shoot that day for a major magazine cover. I knew people were counting on me to show up. I knew calling to cancel, especially so late, would mean losing not just this cover but perhaps any future opportunities with this magazine as well. Makeup artists, stylists, photographers, magazine executives, and even my manager were all going to be disappointed in me and worse.

But I couldn't even face myself that morning. There was no way I could face the cameras. No amount of makeup could have concealed the dark circles and puffy eyelids. After delivering the news to a crew of very unhappy people, I hung up the phone and went straight back to bed. And stayed there for nearly three days.

Apparently, however, even in your darkest hours, *you still have to pee.* On the morning of the third day, as I dragged myself up to use the bathroom yet again, I caught a glimpse of my reflection in the mirror and I had to just stop. It was so eerie. I had no clue who I was looking at. I resembled no one I even knew, let alone my very own self! It was almost as if I were standing outside of my body, looking through the hollow remnants of some person (surely not me) who used to live there.

Never mind the superficial aspects: the puffy eyes, dark circles, matted hair, pasty skin, and really rank sweats—the very core of me, Cindy, myself, was gone.

The Pity Party's Over

In that moment, I realized that I had to be done feeling sorry for myself and pretty darn quick. If I didn't pull myself up and out of this poor-little-me world that I was becoming so comfortable in, I would lose everything. I was really at the edge: To go on like this, I would not only never have a baby, but I would also surely lose my loving husband, my career, and most important, myself. As I stood there looking, one thing became perfectly clear: That person in the mirror looking back at me was *not* the person I wanted to be, *not* the person my husband deserved, *not* the person God would entrust with a new life, for sure.

Looking back, I guess somewhere in the back of my mind I had always had a hunch, call it a sixth sense, that I would not have an easy time at this whole baby thing. In my twenties, so many of my girlfriends went through major pregnancy scares, but I never even had a close call. I was never more than a day or two late with my period, which is amazing since I had a serious boyfriend and, although we tried to practice safe sex, there were many occasions where we threw caution (and all of our clothes) to the wind and just went for it. So I can't say I was overly surprised when it didn't happen for Guy and me right away.

Besides, what was I thinking? I was a fighter. Always had been. And I needed to fight this starting now. So, in that very instant, I shed those depressed feelings (and those nasty, baggy, smelly sweats), cranked the shower up to hot, and stepped inside. It was time to get proactive. First step? A visit to my gynecologist.

I must have sounded deranged when I called my doctor's office later that afternoon because the nurse gave me an appointment the very next morning. Well, I might have put the brakes on the pity party, but I was clearly still in a kind of psycho state. My doctor barely got out a "Hello, Cindy, how can I help you today?" before the story of what had been happening just erupted out of me. The whole year of frustrations, fears, and insecurities. By the time I'd finished I felt as though I had emptied the reservoir of every bad thought and feeling I had for myself and for Guy over the past eighteen months. And with the release of all that pent-up energy, I felt like I finally might be able to fill myself back up with useful knowledge and a plan.

Guy didn't come with me. No one did. I hadn't even told anyone I was going to see the doctor. I was so shaken, so sure that when all was said and done, the fault would be placed on me. I was older than Guy, and this played heavily in even my most rational thoughts as to why this was happening or—more precisely—why it *wasn't* happening. I just couldn't imagine digesting that information with anyone else present but my doctor. Looking back, of course, I see that that was a silly thing to do. I could have used Guy's support in taking that first step. I never excluded him from any part of the process again.

Frankly, I could have also used the support of my gynecologist. Yes, I'm afraid not all doctors are created equal. This particular gynecologist had seen nearly every female member of my family, even some neighbors; so when it was my turn, he was automatically appointed guardian of my gynecological health. But there I was, a nervous wreck, pouring out the entire contents of my heart, and all he asked me were the most superficial questions: "When was your last period?" "How long have you been having unprotected sex?" And "How is your mother, by the way?" *Ugh!*

He moved me through the twenty-minute appointment, offering me precious little insight as to what was happening with

When to Seek Out a Fertility Specialist

- If you are under thirty-five and not conceiving after a few months of trying
- If you are over thirty-five and have not conceived after three to six months of trying
- If you have reason to believe you have blocked fallopian tubes or your husband has low sperm count or other fertility problems
- If you want to quickly check the basics

my body and giving me instructions to see his nurse on the way out for a list of fertility specialists.

This is not how it's supposed to go. I understand that gynecologists are not necessarily fertility specialists, and that my gynecologist is certainly very skilled, but I'm sure there are specific questions he could have asked and information he could have provided in addition to the referrals. He could have tried to calm my anxieties and still a few of my more irrational fears. I was disappointed and confused when he did neither.

Happily, we began to get some answers with our first visit to the fertility specialist. And despite my disappointment with my first doctor's lack of good bedside manner, I still left his office that day—list of fertility specialist referrals in hand—feeling at least a little excited that we might be able to fix this problem.

> What if the fertility specialist said we couldn't have children?

I drove home in a blur. I couldn't wait to show Guy the referral slip that just might prove to be our ticket to baby happiness. But I was also nauseous with the anxiety about what this new person might have to say about our chances of fulfilling our baby dreams. What if he or she said we couldn't have children? What if the fertility specialist said that I had waited too long, was too old, too short, too tall, too fat, too ugly, too silly, not silly enough, or—worse—that there was something so wrong

---

A first visit to the fertility specialist can and should educate and empower you.

with my insides that I should give up my dream of being a mother forever?

On the other hand, what if this fertility specialist could help us? What if this time next year, we could be holding our own precious baby in our arms? What if I *could* become a mother with just a little bit of help? We had to take the chance, didn't we? *I* had to take that chance. I had to take control and *fight* for that chance or hang up my baby booties right now.

CHAPTER 2

The High-Tech
Journey Begins

In a lot of ways, seeing an infertility specialist is like going to an Alcholics Anonymous meeting. You have to admit you have a problem before you can get the help you need. So I did. I admitted it out loud in the car that day and practiced it all the way home. I said it to Guy, to my mother, to my brother, and even to a very astonished clerk at the local drugstore where I had stopped on my way home that afternoon. By the time I had to say it into the phone to the receptionist at the fertility clinic, I could say it loud and proud—and without tears. "Hello," I said. "I'm Cindy Margolis, and I need to see the doctor. I can't get pregnant."

Guy and I met with Dr. Snunit Ben-Ozer of the Tree of Life Center on a bright, sunny Wednesday afternoon. As hopeful as I was on the drive to her office that afternoon for our first visit, I still felt like we were being initiated into the Reproductively Challenged Club. I knew this was one of the best clinics around and that the doctor would be totally professional, but I still felt like Guy and I were wearing T-shirts that announced to the world, "Hey! Look at us! We can't get pregnant!"

But the doctor turned out to be lovely and compassionate, with a very warm bedside manner. She was of slight stature and looked crisp and fresh and somehow all-knowing in her white lab coat. As she greeted us, taking each of our hands in hers, I saw a flicker of renewed hope that our baby dreams might come true. Her smile said, *Don't worry*, her deep brown eyes said, *I will help you.* And as she ushered us to take seats on the couch in her office, our hands still joined, I was so grateful for her that I again started babbling nonstop. She and Guy, meanwhile, sat there patiently, waiting for me to run out of breath.

"I'm so worried," I told her, "that my clock is ticking. In all the articles and books, they tell you that by this point [remember, I had already hit the big three-five] a woman has fewer and fewer eggs each month to contribute to the baby-making process. They also tell you that the eggs you do have are probably poor performers. If I believe only half of everything I've read," I carried on, "my chances of winning the lottery are still greater at this point than us getting pregnant, right?" If you can believe it, I then went on to explain to *her*, the head of one of the most respected fertility centers around, about how a woman's reproductive system works and what I think was or had been wrong with mine since the age of thirteen. I even ventured into man world and told her everything she wanted to know (or didn't!) about Guy's habits, sharing details about semen output and penis behavior, much to the surprise and astonishment of my poor husband, who, as of yet, had been unable to squeeze in more than six words: "Hello, doctor, nice to meet you."

THE HIGH-TECH JOURNEY BEGINS

How to Find a Fertility Specialist in Your Area

It's always best to have a personal referral to a specialist. If your doctor is unable to provide you with one or you want to check out your options, there are a number of good websites that list fertility resources by city or region. I find the following to be the most reliable:

Society for Assisted Reproductive Technology
www.sart.org

The American Fertility Association
888-917-3777
www.theafa.org

Internet Health Resources
www.ihr.com
This website has links to infertility specialists in every region of the country, as well as egg and sperm donors and surrogacy services.

There was a lot of nodding and note taking going on throughout my impromptu refresher course on human sexuality and reproductive systems, and I still think I must have impressed her with my wide variety of research and knowledge in this area! Guy maybe not so much. But then he was probably still wondering how I could possibly so nonchalantly share such intimate details about his little buddy with a complete stranger.

At any rate, the note taking finally stopped, and another warm smile came across the doctor's face as she asked us to provide her with the details of our health histories and our ages. I hated this part because I would have to confess that I was the old one in this relationship. Guy is five years younger than I am, and I closely studied her face to see if she would immediately recognize this as *the* problem in our conception efforts and pass judgment on just who was at fault.

"It's me, isn't it?" I wanted to scream. "Go ahead and say it: 'You're the problem, Cindy, because you simply waited too long. You're too old and therefore no longer have the ability to make baby eggs!' "

Very often your gynecologist will have some basic training in fertility testing and perhaps even in providing minimal treatment. But if you are experiencing difficulties, it is always best to go to a fertility specialist. Sometimes it's worthwhile to have even just one consultation or appointment to educate yourself.

What to Look for in a Fertility Specialist
- A feeling of connection and support
- A compassionate and informative staff and doctor
- Thorough and respectful answers to your questions
- Board certification
- Reasonable success rates (you can check the Centers for Disease Control and Prevention's website, www.cdc.gov, for more information)
- Convenient office hours
- Convenient location, at least as you are getting started
- No hassle getting an appointment

But Dr. Ben-Ozer gently reached for my hand, looked at me knowingly, and positively reassured me that thirty-five is by no means ancient. She explained that I probably still had eggs aplenty and that we could, we *would*, get to the bottom of the problem. She spoke plainly as she explained that there would be hard decisions ahead and a potentially rocky road, for sure, but that we would take it one step at a time.

The first step? A question: Did Guy and I want to keep trying naturally or were we at the point at which we might want to take a more aggressive approach to starting our family? I couldn't bear the thought of going possibly several more years without a baby, and believe me, continuing to have baby-possessed sex was not all that appealing either. With one knowing look between us, we turned to the doctor and said in unison, "We'll take door number two."

We took a few deep, cleansing breaths and scheduled our next appointment—along with the first set of testing procedures in what would soon become an endless routine of testing.

It felt good to put myself in someone else's hands. There was a certain amount of immediate comfort in the fact that our doctor was so experienced in this field and had seen hundreds of other couples going through these same problems. I remember feeling kind of overwhelmed when I was first given a list of specialists. How on earth would we be able to choose the right doctor for us? We checked the credentials of each and every one. Researched them and their clinics on the Internet, asked to talk to people they had previously treated, and then began making interview appointments. Dr. Ben-Ozer was just the second doctor we interviewed, but I felt an immediate connection with her, and I think Guy did, too. She made us feel comfortable, and there was a

Your Basic Infertility Workup

In the old days (until the past few years), women used to chart their basal body temperature (before taking a step out of bed in the morning) over the course of every month to determine if they were biphasal, which is a good indication of normal ovulation. Today we have better tools. A basic infertility workup involves the following:

- A detailed history and physical of both partners
- A semen analysis
- Hysterosalpingography (HSG): Dye is injected into the uterus, and radiology is used to follow it as it travels up into the fallopian tubes; this determines if the tubes are blocked in any way.
- A measure of progesterone levels: determines if ovulation is happening normally
- An evaluation of the woman's endocrine function: for example, a thyroid function test and a measure of prolactin, estrogen, and/or testosterone levels
- A measure of other critical fertility-related hormone levels: for example, estradiol (EA) and follicle-stimulating hormone (FSH)

chemistry between us, and not only because she was a woman. I'd had women doctors before. No, I think this had more to do with the fact that she was obviously a woman who truly cared about how we were going to get through this. That feeling of connection and trust became very important as we had to open up and share our most intimate thoughts and behaviors with her.

On the way out, I scanned the waiting room. It was standing-room only. Could there actually be this many women having the same problem as I was? Obviously, the answer was yes. I admit, I felt better. Because for the first time since this long journey began, I didn't feel as if Guy and I were alone. I didn't feel hopeless, and I didn't feel we had to solve this problem on our own.

We had just taken a positive first step. We would do *every-thing* it took, and we wouldn't complain.

I glanced around the waiting room one last time, looking more closely into the faces of the men and women. I saw myself over and over in the frazzled, frightened, sad, and confused expressions. I wondered just how many happy endings there would be in this room, and if Guy and I would be one of them.

You see, it doesn't matter how famous you are, how you look, or what your socioeconomic status is: Infertility issues can happen to anyone. In fact, in that year alone, I would later find out, more than 10 million couples were on that same roller coaster ride of oh-so-monotonous, nonstop, nonsatisfying sex and still coming up empty in the baby department. I'll bet most of them were also thinking, just as I was, "Why us?"

Your First Assignment

Here's your first assignment. Tell your doctor that you're having trouble getting pregnant. If it's been more than six months or a year, ask for a referral to a specialist. Then, put together a list of questions you want to ask at your first appointment.

And just remember, you aren't really wearing a T-shirt that says, "Look at us, we can't get pregnant." Apparently, you actually have to *tell* the doctor you can't get pregnant. Go figure!

Know Your Body

I can't stress enough how important it is to get to know your body and how your particular body changes throughout your menstrual cycle. Beyond the frantic sex, you need to understand the signs of impending ovulation. News flash—we don't all work exactly the same. Oh yeah, the basics are all there, but believe me, knowing how *your* body operates will make you more comfortable and help you predict the ideal time for sex, which of course will maximize your odds of getting a successfully fertilized egg.

But in addition, the more information you can share with your doctor about *your* body the better. Infertility testing is slow. It can take months for the doctor to run all the necessary tests, analyze the results, and find the perfect method of treating you. You can speed things along tremendously by preparing ahead of time.

Walk in each month with your temperature charts, ovulation predictor kits, and your cervical mucus in hand. (Well, maybe not the mucus. But you get the idea.) The better prepared you are, the easier it will go. Many women can actually *feel* when they ovulate. This is a mixed blessing for sure. It's great when you're trying to get pregnant, but it can also send you to the hospital thinking you're having an acute appendicitis attack each month! The beau-

---

Remember, if you have any fertility concerns at all, you can choose to go to a reproductive endocrinologist and infertility (REI) specialist for a consultation at any time, which can really empower you and reduce your levels of stress as you face the unknown.

---

tiful thing is, you don't have to guess. Get yourself acquainted with the advanced "pee on the stick" technology now available in wonderful little miracle ovulation strips, and learn how to use them accurately. Afraid of peeing on your hand? Then try the TCI Ovulation Tester, which predicts ovulation by testing your saliva. Either is a great tool when added to your own intuition.

Oh yes, and don't forget to explore your vagina. *Know* how it feels before you become pregnant so you will be alerted to the changes that can aid your pregnancy efforts. For instance, when you ovulate, your cervical mucus thickens and gets kind of stringy to better assist in transporting your partner's sperm to your eggs. If you're attuned to this change in your mucus, you can better predict the optimal time to have sex.

The change in the shape of your cervix is also another early sign to be aware of. If you've never sat down and had a real girl-to-girl with your vagina, now is the time. Plop down in a comfy chair, get out a good-size mirror, and take a look. This is the doorway to the new home you are preparing for your precious baby. You better know everything you can about how it looks, how it feels, and how it's going to act—before you try to place your baby inside. What you know could in fact be the difference between whether your baby stays there for eight days or for forty weeks. *That's* how important this is.

Okay, So What *Is* Wrong?
Tests, Procedures, Diagnosis

At this point, Guy and I had been trying to get pregnant on our own for about two years. We were actually kind of relieved to be at the testing stage, and approached our initial tests with optimism and an eagerness that surprised no one—at least no one who knew me very well. We were more sure now. More confident. Not only in our doctor but also in our faith and in the knowledge that we were on the right track to getting the help we needed. So eager was I, that I insisted on being tested not just for the normal things, not just for those few things that may be considered outside the normal things . . . but for *everything*. In fact, there are those who might even now say I was a lunatic about it.

It seemed then, and now, perfectly reasonable to me that if a woman from a tribe in Africa became infertile because she ate berries that are found only in the deepest forests of Argentina, well then, my doctor would surely want to test me for that as well! If there was a one in a million chance that one of us carried a gene for a rare genetic disease, I wanted to be tested for that, too. In fact, if an alien had landed or had plans of landing on earth anytime within the next few months that *we* were trying to get pregnant, and there were any possibility that this alien would bring a germ that could prevent our baby from being born, I wanted our doctor to somehow, some way, figure out a way (if you please) to test us for that too! And so it went.

Test after test after test—until finally, *aha*, we might have found the reason not only for our current problems but also for all those years of painful periods. Or that's what we thought when we were first presented with a diagnosis of endometriosis. Halle-

---

You may want to discuss with your gynecologist the benefits of getting preconception and prepregnancy genetic testing.

---

lujah! Could this be it? Could it really be that simple? "How soon can we fix this and be on our way to more successful baby making?" we asked. We were told we could do laparoscopic surgery (which doesn't involve large incisions), and after a short period of healing just try again.

I was so excited. So much so, that—despite the doctor's careful warnings, despite all her efforts to remind us that it was still early and there were no guarantees—we actually looked forward to the surgery. Maybe unblocking my plumbing was the answer we had been waiting for.

Unfortunately, it was not. While my endometriosis definitely needed to be treated, it was, it seemed, not the only obstacle in our path. It was also not our "specific diagnosis." But more on that later.

Infertility is one of those words that covers a very wide range of medical, emotional, and often unexplainable issues and reasons that keep couples from getting pregnant. You hear the word all the time, but what does it really mean? Doctors specializing in infertility consider a couple to be infertile if one of these three statements is true:

What Is Endometriosis?

Endometriosis occurs when tissue that normally lines the uterus is found in other parts of the body, usually in the pelvic cavity, where it can hinder the function of the fallopian tubes and thereby cause infertility. Some patients with endometriosis suffer great pain during their periods or throughout the month.

- The couple has not conceived after twelve months of unprotected intercourse if the woman is under the age of thirty-five.

- The couple has not conceived after six months of unprotected intercourse if the woman is over the age of thirty-five.

- The woman is incapable of carrying a baby to term.

Not very precise, is it?

What we were to discover from Dr. Ben-Ozer is that while there are many causes of infertility among men and women between the ages of twenty and forty-five, only about 40 percent of the time is it female related. Another 30 percent can be attributed to the male partner, and another 20 percent involves both partners. Which leaves the final 10 percent "unexplained."

There are many causes of infertility among men and women between the ages of twenty and forty-five. About 40 percent of the time the problem is female related. Another 30 percent can be attributed to the male partner, and another 20 percent involves both partners. About 10 percent go unexplained.

Common Causes of Infertility
- Male factor infertility
- Ovulatory factor (polycystic ovarian syndrome)
- Tubal factor (blocked tubes)
- Uterine factor (Asherman's syndrome)
- Endometriosis
- Other (immunological, endocrine, etc.)

Male Factor Infertility

The infertility stigma is almost always discussed in terms of female issues, but the truth is, male factor infertility is more common than you would imagine. Even among those of us who are willing to discuss our infertility publicly, you will not find many men—and even fewer men of celebrity status—willing to admit that the problem is in their court.

Of course Guy sweated a little early on at the possibility that it was his sperm that was causing our fertility problems. As it turns out, it wasn't. But plenty of men and couples do have to struggle with male infertility, which can have many causes, from other health issues, such as cancers, to the inability to ejaculate to suboptimal semen quality, low sperm counts, vas deferens obstruction, exposure to environmental toxins or drugs, the presence of a large varicocele (an enlargement of the veins in the scrotum), cryptorchidism (undescended testes—one or both, which should always be surgically corrected to prevent testicular cancer), or chromosomal abnormality.

In addition, existing health complications of infertile men, especially among older males, can also dramatically affect treatment and available options. Cancers, diabetes, heart disease, and blood pressure diseases, among others, can wreak havoc when combined with the normal stresses of a couple trying to conceive.

New procedures like intracytoplasmic sperm injection (ICSI) are revolutionizing the treatment of male infertility, making it possible to assist sperm in fertilizing a woman's eggs. Not all men can be helped by ICSI, but it's a great advance. Unfortunately it's still an IVF-based procedure and requires

These days you can buy an over-the-counter test for men to check their sperm count. This is certainly a positive development for infertile couples. It should be noted, however, that this test is very basic and doesn't test fertility. It only measures sperm concentration—without any indication of potential problems with the sperms' ability to fertilize an egg or even whether the seminal fluid contains antisperm antibodies.

For young couples who are early on in their fertility journey, and have no reason to suspect fertility problems, this test could be helpful. If, however, you are older or have been trying to conceive for more than six months, or younger and have been at it for more than a year, this test is no substitute for consultation with a fertility specialist. In fact it can provide false reassurance and postpone your search for professional help and thereby delay your pregnancy or other decisions regarding starting your family.

For more information about the test, you can go to www .testcountry.com and search for "male fertility test" in the search bar.

that both partners be treated (nope, you don't get out of hormone hell just yet, ladies), but it takes only about sixty extra seconds. (*Hmmmm*, even male infertility is measured in minutes, not days or weeks or months. Some days it definitely sucks to be us.)

Our friends Nancy and Daniel have been struggling with his very low sperm count for some time. They have been trying ICSI, in which the doctor can take just one sperm and inject it into the egg to maximize the chances of fertilization. It also involves putting the woman through IVF, so both partners really go for a ride on this one:

In some ways, we're a lot like other infertile couples. We share the same pain, the hopes and fears, and the ups and downs of treatment. But in some ways, we're a bit different. For one, male factor is particularly hard on the man involved. Daniel has a lot of unresolved feelings that he doesn't really want to talk about, and that sometimes makes it hard for us to keep communications open. I find that IVF dominates my life when I'm in treatment. I want to talk about the IVF and our different options and what we'll do if we fail, but he just avoids the topic. That makes me feel as if I were isolated and misunderstood—after all, we're infertile together!

On his side, I think he feels that I'm not sufficiently aware of how traumatic his experiences have been—for him, talking about IVF now is like raking up all the miserable tests and things that led to his diagnosis way back when. This communication gap has really caused problems for us, and only now are we working things out a bit.

Sometimes I feel guilty when talking to my many wonderful cycle buddies (CBs) who have female factor problems. These strong women have been through so much, and I have not. (This is my own perception, not any guilt they lay on me. My CBs have always been outstandingly supportive of one another, whatever the diagnosis.)

Trying to see the silver lining, I would say that the failure of our first IVF has made us stronger as a couple. It really forced us to confront our failures of communication and try to set up ways to do better in the future. This wasn't instantaneous, or easy. It meant long days (and nights) of hurt feelings, and a few really awful fights.

Resources on Male Infertility

The Men's Room
Go to www.inciid.org and follow the chat links.
A chat room for men about men's issues and infertility concerns offered by the InterNational Council on Infertility Information Dissemination (INCIID, pronounced *Inside*).

Internet Health Resources
www.ihr.com/infertility/male.html
A comprehensive site for many issues related to infertility, with a page devoted to male infertility and links to resources on treatment.

But we are facing our second IVF with a better attitude, and a much more open atmosphere. This time, we are really ready!

The Diagnosis: Surviving the Shock

After six months of tests and several procedures, we were diagnosed with unexplained infertility. In reality, *unexplained* means nothing more than "it can't be diagnosed," which really means that it's not our fault at all. Knowing that, however, did nothing to make either me or Guy feel better about our situation. In fact, hearing the official diagnosis of our infertility almost sent me back to my bed. "How can you not know what's wrong with us? What do you mean there's no medical explanation for our inability to conceive? What's that all about? Wasn't that the whole point of test after test after test? What were these last few months about?"

I was crushed. It may sound crazy, but if you're going through this nightmare (or even if you've ever had some other mysterious medical affliction), you'll know what I'm talking about. I needed to know what was wrong. I needed my doctor to find that *something* was wrong. *Anything!* You see, with something wrong I could at least have surgery or take a pill to make me better. Something—so we could move on to the happier part where we get the baby. Right?

Rationally, I knew from all my reading and research that as many as 10 percent of all couples struggling with infertility receive this diagnosis, but it was still a devastating blow. Dr. Ben-Ozer then said words we didn't want to hear. She told us that it might take years for me to become pregnant naturally, if ever. Of course she also explained that the technology was very promising and that we would probably have a great shot with some of the high-tech interventions. My heart still sank.

It would have been easy at this point to turn inside ourselves and go home to lick our wounds. Guy could bury himself in his work, and I could crawl back into our bed, pull the covers over my head, and cry myself to sleep for the next thirty years. That's certainly what I felt like doing. But that would have been exactly the wrong thing to do right then. And if this is the diagnosis you are facing, I have to tell you, communication between partners is the key to getting through this and the many other heartbreaks and setbacks that lie ahead for you. This is not an easy situation, and you need to talk to each other even when what you really feel like doing is never talking to your partner again!

One of the realities of infertility is that many women crave the feeling of being pregnant and, therefore, tend to feel the loss more acutely when we can't conceive. I know men feel it, but for many reasons they react differently and usually less outwardly. They may even feel the same sense of loss, but often they don't have the same outlets for expressing their confusion, embarrassment, or fears. This can leave them pretty resentful about the way women throw themselves into the process and turn their lives over to getting pregnant. Even in instances in which low sperm count or sluggish sperm mobility is clearly the only issue, men often won't step up to the plate as readily or as eagerly as a woman probably would in an effort to resolve the situation and get to the baby part.

Regardless of your particular diagnosis, however, there are many choices for you and your partner to begin making at this point. You're going to start receiving a lot of information about medicines and tests and procedures. You need to stay focused so you can accept and sort through all the information, but you also have to stay together on this so you know what to expect of each other as you evaluate your options. You need to know what the other is feeling and resist that urge to feel alone and hurt by misspoken words about issues you're both still trying hard to understand.

Nearly one in six adults of childbearing age has infertility issues. You are not alone!

Keeping Open the Lines of Communication with Your Mate

- **Find time when you're least likely to be interrupted.** Try not to do this when you're very tired.

- **Talk about the specific options available to you now that your testing is over and you have your diagnosis.** How do you think your specific diagnosis is going to affect your relationship, your day-to-day life, your decisions from this point on?

- **Give each other the opportunity to talk about your individual jobs, career, family, and financial goals.** See if you're still on the same page with each other's thoughts, and discuss and resolve outstanding issues in these areas. Agree to disagree where you must, but do not leave things hanging in the areas that matter most to you.

- **Talk about your religious beliefs.** Will they affect some of the choices you'll be making as you seek help to conceive?

- **Decide whether you will tell or not tell family and friends.** And then, how much you will tell and when you will tell it.

- **Really devote yourselves to finding out specifically how the other thinks in these critical areas before you have to face them together.**

- **Remind each other—and yourselves—that none of this is your fault and there are no easy fixes!**

These are all very important topics. Try to talk about them every day, or at least once a week. The sooner you start thinking and talking about them, the easier it will be to draw material from these discussions during subsequent doctor visits. *Be sure to relate your feelings and decisions to your doctor,* so your treatments can be best tailored for you.

Infertility is as much about survival as it is about success. I can't tell you how important it is to stay focused on your baby dreams and not on your own personal hurts and disappointments. You need to think of yourselves as a team playing for the biggest trophy in the world. When your teammate is down or hurting, you do not lash out, throw him or her to the ground, and stomp on his or her feelings.

Take turns. Provide comfort, diversion, and—most important—a little bit of humor and love, especially in those times when that's the *last* thing on your mind. Because that's when it will matter most. I was lucky. Guy didn't let me wallow in my poor-me state any longer than it took for him to dry my tears. Now don't misunderstand. He didn't deny me those tears. To do so wouldn't have given me the chance to work through my feelings. But he would quickly pat my face dry and send me on my way to our next appointment, our next test, the next shot, the next hurdle. Oh yeah, it's all about survival, baby. One step at a time.

Here's where your doctor can also make a big, big difference, too. Dr. Ben-Ozer spent a lot of time with us explaining the road ahead, and I think that made surviving the process a lot easier because we weren't always forging ahead into darkness.

See a Specialist

Get yourself properly diagnosed. In some cases, your problems can and will be solved surgically (a simple unblocking of your fallopian tubes, for instance)—and you'll be happily on your way and pregnant, with fewer obstacles and heartaches than the rest of us. Often, however, there will be a few more hoops for you to jump through before that happy day. Guy and I, for example, had to deal first with the unexplained infertility diagnosis. That was hoop number one. We needed to get past the fact that our problem was not an easy fix before we could even think about the options available to us to fix it. Or maybe it was just me who needed to do that.

Getting Used to the Stick

If you are squeamish about needles and blood draws, you're just going to have to get over it. Whatever it takes, do it. In the diagnosing phase alone, you will start to feel like a human pincushion. One thing you can do for sure is ask to lie down. You often aren't told this, but you're much less likely to get faint if your blood is drawn while you are supine. I also know women who have brought stuffed animals along to their blood draws and held them tight as the needle goes in. It really helps!

The other piece of cheery news I have for you is that there are lots and lots and *lots* of shots involved in this process. If you're lucky, your husband or partner may do the deed. But if you're like the majority of women facing a diagnosis of infertility, chances are you'll be giving most, if not all, of the shots to yourself. Granted, these aren't the kind you need to be a nurse to give. It's not like getting your blood taken. The needles don't go into veins. They go into muscle. But it is still not a fun day at the park. At the suggestion of her doctor, one of our friends practiced injecting an orange to get used to the feeling of sticking a needle into flesh. Of course it's a little different when it's your own arm or rear end, but she says the practice really helped.

A Crash Course in Pregnancy Hormones

In the normal course of a monthly cycle, your hormone levels naturally fluctuate within certain acceptable ranges. Two hormones in particular play critical roles: luteinizing hormone (LH), which is directly involved in ovulation, and follicle-stimulating hormone (FSH), which stimulates the maturation of one or two (or more) of the thousands of eggs present in our ovaries from birth. If you are ovulating normally, a surge of LH will trigger the release of the egg (ovulation), which has been maturing under the steady rise of FSH over the course of your cycle. What you're looking for here are low FSH values, which mean the ovary is sensitive and has a good chance of having a large ovarian reserve (lots of good eggs).

An LH surge indicates a woman's most fertile time and helps time intercourse or insemination. Increased FSH levels correlate with ovarian reserve (the ability to produce eggs) and quantity.

Deficiencies or excesses of either hormone will make getting pregnant that much harder. That's why both hormones are usually tested frequently during infertility diagnosis and treatment. The good news is, they can often be boosted effectively with medication.

The other hormone you will hear a lot about as you try to get pregnant is human chorionic gonadotropin (hCG). This hormone is normally produced only during pregnancy and is produced within the embryo shortly after conception to help keep your progesterone (another pregnancy hormone) levels high enough to sustain the pregnancy. In fact, early pregnancy tests indicate the presence of hCG. The very presence of it means that you are pregnant.

Women who are undergoing fertility treatments (more on this in a later chapter) are often given a shot of hCG (get ready—right in the haunch!) to trigger ovulation. Ovulation usually occurs thirty-six to forty-four hours after the injection.

The First Line of Treatments

By the time you have your baby, you will feel like a pharmacist, you will know so much about fertility drugs and what they do. Here are the ones you're sure to hear about:

Clomid (generic name: clomiphene citrate)   Clomid is usually the first fertility drug you will be offered, often starting with something called the "Clomid challenge." The Clomid Challenge tests both your body's ability to make eggs and their quality. Clomid (don't worry, this one's just an easy-to-swallow, relatively inexpensive pill) is also used as a treatment to induce ovulation. We don't know how, exactly, but it seems to fool the body into producing more of each of the hormones involved in getting pregnant. I went positively berserk on Clomid, turning into a raving lunatic. Lots of women describe it as "raging PMS." Doctors believe that this is because Clomid briefly causes the brain to sense very low levels of estrogen, sometimes in the menopausal range (more on this later). Some women feel no negative effects at all, bless their souls.

Repronex, Menopur, or Humegon Repronex, Menopur, or Humegon is often the second drug therapy in the arsenal. More accurately, each of these is a hormone therapy. The drugs actually contain the hormones FSH and LH, which are responsible for stimulating growth and maturation of the egg. Each is administered by injection, either subcutaneously or intramuscularly. Lucky you, your spouse can learn how to administer the shot. The drug would be followed up by hCG to trigger ovulation.

Follistim, Gonal-F, or Bravelle Follistim, Gonal-F, and Bravelle are also given by injection. Each of these is FSH alone and is used in conjunction with hCG to increase the number of eggs produced and thereby enhance fertility.

The Crashing Conclusion to a Lifelong Fantasy

I used to picture myself taking one of those home pregnancy tests, having it come up positive, and spending the rest of the day planning how I was going to break the happy news first to my husband and then to my family. None of the zillions of fantasies I imagined over the years, however, included a sterile examining room, a microscope, or looking expectantly at a doctor who was wearing a lab coat and pushing a catheter up my vagina. I can't imagine it being a part of any woman's baby dreams.

So when it became a part of mine, and Guy needed me to move into "medically assisted pregnancy" mode, I resisted with all my heart. I wanted to maintain the fantasy as long as possible, because letting it go was not just scary to me, it was downright bone chilling. We had now come this far, however, and there was no turning back.

CHAPTER 3

Here's a *Playboy*—Go Make Me Some Sperm! Or Let's Get Clinical

It was a great blow to my ego not to be able to get pregnant, and perhaps an even greater blow to my sense of general fairness (not to mention sense of control) that no one could tell us why. So, with a somewhat heavier than expected heart, we consciously and officially made the choice to turn our baby dreams over to science. This meant that we were also agreeing that *our* baby business was now going to be *everybody's* baby business. I was so out of my mind at this point, that not telling family and friends would surely have them calling the nearest mental facility and trying to have me involuntarily committed.

It may seem odd to those of you who haven't been there but, like a pregnant woman who develops strange food cravings, infertile women can develop pretty unusual behaviors, too. If the hormones don't induce it (which they will, believe me), the deluge of

Strange behaviors and rituals usually become a routine part of daily life when you're trying to get pregnant.

crazy thoughts running through your head both day and night surely will. Strange behaviors, rituals, nesting, gathering, and almost any other unusual or unnatural act you can think of can (and often does) actually become part of a routine day in the life of an infertile woman trying to get pregnant.

For me, it was an insatiable need for information. It was a coping thing. The more I read, the better I felt—because information would help explain what was going on inside my body, and I was sure that would equal having more control over what it did or didn't do. Of course, that wasn't really true, but the fantasy remained with me throughout our repeated attempts to conceive. So much so, in fact, that I have a special little tip for you hubbies out there: If you ever feel the urge to point out that your mate is being irrational, don't!

A woman who is being pumped full of enough hormones to turn Glinda the Good Witch into Arnold the Terminator is just not the person you want to criticize. Just shut up, write it in a journal, tell your buddies down at the office, or complain to your mother. Believe me, those are much safer options.

And so it was that Guy and I took our first stab (yes, literally) at artificial insemination. Our first efforts would be with intra-uterine inseminations (IUIs), which are much easier and cheaper than in vitro fertilization (IVF) and are usually the first intervention recommended. (Don't worry, we'll get to that later.) We knew that Guy's sperm were hearty and could swim straight and that I had no obstructions in my fallopian tubes and my hormones were rising and falling each month just like they were supposed to do, so the next step was to give them all a little boost. With an IUI, the doctor takes your partner's sperm (which he has so graciously provided after masturbating to porn), washes it to prevent severe intrauterine cramping, maximize quality of the sperm, reduce the distance the sperm need to travel to fertilize the egg, and allow freezing for later use. She then injects it directly into your uterus with a very small, flexible, and soft catheter. This apparently increases the chances that the little swimmers will make it to their destination without getting sidetracked in the vagina or cervix.

Maniac for reading that I was, I would study the process late into the night, often falling asleep with an open book splayed across my chest in an effort to understand how to do it right the first time. When it came time for our first procedure, however, I wound up feeling like I totally got the short end of the stick. Or was it the long end? For stick is surely what I got! Throughout the process, I was stuck with so many needles I thought I would leak like a sieve the next time I drank anything. Guy on the other hand, was offered a couple copies of *Playboy*, sent to a room where they played nonstop porn movies, and told to "fill a cup."

Not fair! He gets to go look at sexy women who are *not* me, and I get to put my feet up in stirrups and have a cold speculum rammed into my vagina? Of course, Guy will tell you how difficult it was for him to perform on demand like that, especially since he could hear a bunch of sixty-year-old nurses talking outside the "performance room," but I think you ladies will agree that the inequities are clear. I wanted to get pregnant at all costs, but I just never pictured conceiving our child in separate rooms, with my husband looking not at me but at an X-rated video. This was not how it was supposed to go.

> *This is the part where making love becomes making a baby.*

It's also a very difficult thing to overcome for many couples, so I would urge you to spend some time talking about this before your first procedure. If there is such a thing as a defining moment, in which you really feel like you've turned your life over to science, this is it. Or at least it was for me. This is the part where making love became making a baby—and believe me, it is not the same thing. It's a job. It's work. It's *hard* work, and you can put those notions of passion and intimacy on the shelf. You will not need them again until *after* your child is born (at which point they may have to stay on the shelf until you adjust to the new noises in your household).

What Happens to the Sex?

Guy and I really treasured our sexual relationship and our intimate and romantic moments together, but it was time to trade in that model for a more practical seminal fluid–delivery system. At this point and until we had our first child, our sex quickly became perfunctory. Almost a chore. The worst part of it: carrying a load of stress and pressure that you will not believe possible until you're actually in the midst of it. It was all about timing, cycles, and sperm.

Following each round of penetration at home, and throughout the whole medically assisted process, I would make Guy hold my legs up in the air for a full thirty minutes. Someone had told me that gravity works against the sperm staying up there and that headstands would help. Well, I'm no gymnast, but holding my legs up in the air was something we could do. Again, not as much fun as it sounds!

Once, realizing that I was about to ovulate and we were nowhere near the clinic for an insemination, we even had sex in the backseat of Guy's car, only a few feet off the exit ramp and probably in plain view of anyone who was interested.

My legs had been in the air only twenty minutes when an inquisitive policeman pulled up behind us and started sauntering our way. Leaving my ankles propped against a partially rolled up window, my feet dangling freely, I pushed Guy out of the vehicle to go deal with the cop, buying me the ten extra minutes I needed to be sure we hadn't wasted the effort.

Actually, we did go to great lengths to keep things fun and interesting. A few times we sneaked away to a hotel because, of course, there is nothing hotter than hotel sex, right? Or we would take turns trying to come up with cute, sexy, and totally romantic scenarios to play off of throughout the day so that our nights would be more passionate. But no matter what we did or how hard we tried (or maybe *because of* how hard we tried), in the back of our minds was always how much was at stake— trying to start our family just took all the fun out of sex.

Going Public

To make matters worse, I needed someone to share the intimate details of this emotional roller coaster with. Someone to talk to. To discuss all this craziness with. My doctor was there for the medical and procedural questions, but I really needed someone who could tell me what was next and what emotional hurdle

Some of the Obnoxious Things People Will Say—Whether They Mean Well or Not

You're obviously not ready to conceive.
You're too stressed. Maybe if you relax ...
Oh, my husband just has to look at me and I get pregnant!
This must not be the right time.
Come on! Tell me it isn't fun having all that sex!
Maybe you don't really *want* a baby.
When you're ready, it will happen.
If you just stop trying so hard, it will happen.
Not everyone is supposed to be a mother.
You have everything else—do you really need kids, too?
You don't have time for children anyway.
I know somebody just like you who ...

Some of the Things You Can Say Back

Thank you, but that's really not helpful.
Imagine how it would feel if someone said that to *you*!
Thanks, but I'm not looking for advice.
Back off!

we'd be approaching before we actually got there. Someone to warn me about the toll this was going to take on our marriage, and someone to tell me that eventually I really would (someday) enjoy sex with my husband again. I was often tired, confused, and frustrated, but infertility just isn't something people like to chat about openly over dinner. "You know, I'm having a hard time getting knocked up. And how's your filet mignon?" Seriously, I had trouble finding someone I could talk to.

In fact—and I hear this from other women all the time—people end up saying the most God-awful things to you when they hear you're having trouble getting pregnant. They usually mean well (but sometimes they definitely don't), and you should be prepared to hear some really annoying remarks and to get some real stabs to the heart.

Guy and I were doing *everything* right, and I was still not pregnant after the first round of IUIs. We did the ovulation kits, took the hormones, followed all the instructions to the letter—I even took my shots at the same time every day, never deviating from our doctors' directives in even the most minor way, and yet we were no closer to conceiving a child than we were after that two weeks of hot sex on our honeymoon. To say that I was shocked would be the understatement of the year. I was devastated. How could this be? I had read everything possible, had followed the instructions of our infertility specialist to the letter, now knew more about the *inside* of my body than God did, so why weren't we pregnant? I felt like the whole world was having babies (without even trying) and here we were still struggling to get it right. It was hard not to be depressed.

Babies, Babies Everywhere

It seemed like every couple we knew was outfitting a nursery in anticipation of a blessed event in their household. I tried to be happy for them, but I mostly felt as if my heart were breaking into tiny pieces and that with each bit of happy baby news from someone else, another little part of my own heart got washed away forever. Baby shower invitations came in the mail (what

seemed like) almost weekly. They expected me to go celebrate?
To watch as tiny layettes were unwrapped amid the *ooohs*
and *ahhhs* of joyful mommies to be? What kind of cruel world
was I living in?

Sometimes, in my more charming moments, I even found
myself wishing that harm would come to some of my more
smug friends ("Oh, my husband just has to *look* at me, and I get
pregnant!" "I think we'll have our next baby in June, so I can
take the summer off to be with
her!"). I wish someone had told
me how normal this all was. Instead, I walked around feeling like
a total shrew. Now I know that women around the world would
have gladly joined in my whine fest. It *isn't* fair, it brings up the
craziest feelings of rage, and it's often the first time in your life
when you feel so completely out of control.

> I wish someone had told me
> how normal this all was.

At Times Like This, Men Really Are from Mars

Meanwhile, Guy and I were just on different planets. I consider
Guy my soul mate. I truly do. But during this time in our lives I
wondered more often that not, "Does he have any idea what I'm
feeling? Does he even care?" We argued almost daily. For no
reason and for every reason. Men and women often have different ways of expressing their emotions. I think Guy and I were
rather classic examples. I vented everything. I screamed, hollered, cried, threw fits, and issued ultimatums. And when none

of those things worked, I would retreat to my office or our bedroom and try to think up new ways to vent, new words to hurl.

Guy simply became silent. He didn't talk to me unless he had to and didn't give out any more information than was necessary, lest I have a comment or question that might prolong the discussion. We were both hurting and hurting down deep. This was by far the toughest thing that we had ever been through individually or as a couple. Only time would tell if we would come through this still in love with each other.

While we were still having lots of sex, we were both getting angrier all the time that business was not being conducted properly. It put a terrible strain on our relationship, and I was afraid most of the time that our love would sour as we were reaching to embrace the one thing we seemed to want more than each other.

The irony of trying to attain happiness in this type of environment was not lost on either of us. As we learned only much later, Guy and I were, of course, not the first couple to have these thoughts or to silently suffer with doubts too scary to voice, even to each other. Most couples going through infertility at one time or another face these same doubts

Guy and I were, of course, not the first couple to have these thoughts.

and often question the strength of their relationship. The person you thought you knew intimately only a few short months before can suddenly become a stranger. Or at least, that's what you think.

As you go through the process of making a family, you will wonder at least once a week how much of yourself can you actually lose before you've gone beyond the point of no return. The stories of my girlfriends Shelly and Veronica will make you reevaluate your definition of loss. Shelly underwent IUIs and, after many attempts, became pregnant and had a baby boy. Her sister, Veronica, tried for years and was not successful, even after several rounds of IVF. Two sisters, same family, different outcomes. Strange world.

Shelly's Story: Some for Me but Not for You!

I always thought getting pregnant and starting a family would be easy. The family I come from is very large. I am the third child of four and have nineteen first cousins. Our grandparents, aunts, and uncles were traditional Catholics from Indiana. They got married and started having children right away. After fifteen years of it, my parents decided that that lifestyle was not for them, and they divorced when I was ten. The radical changes that came with a divorce, custody, moving, stepfamilies, and an entirely new lifestyle were overwhelming. No one cared what the kids thought or felt, and we were ignored. I wanted children one day, but not the way my parents had me. I wanted to wait until the time was right.

To make a very long story short, I was married twice and divorced twice before I hit twenty-nine. I never wanted children from either husband because both situations were very wrong. Soon I was going full force in my career and loving every minute of it. Life was good but, except for my cats, I was alone. I started seeing Brad when I was thirty and almost right away we started talking about children. It did not frighten him. He was almost thirty-five when we met and he wanted them, too. Almost exactly two years later, we were married.

We knew we would be moving around a lot as Brad finished up his medical training, so we didn't start trying right away. In the fall of 2002, I had a miscarriage. That same year I lost my dad, my grandmother, and a beloved family pet. It was almost too much to bear.

We didn't try again until the summer of 2003, the year I turned thirty-four.

Nothing happened. The months went by, and we had one positive pregnancy test, but my period came the next day. Apparently, I had had a "chemical pregnancy." [Implantation takes place but is quickly followed by a miscarriage.] I kept telling myself that babies come when they are supposed to. More months went by. I turned thirty-five that June and went to see my new obstetrician, and she referred me to a reproductive endocrinologist in her practice. By then, we had been trying for at least a year, and [the endocrinologist] told me he was going to run fertility tests. He would also have me try Clomid, a fertility drug that should help me have a stronger ovulation. I was willing to try whatever he prescribed. From June until August we ran tests, and everything came back normal. Even the ultrasounds of my ovaries and uterine lining revealed healthy and normal anatomy.

The doctor instructed me to take the Clomid, chart my basal body temperature to make sure I was ovulating, and to use the ovulation predictor kit. The Clomid dried up my cervical mucus and made me crazy. I would cry over really stupid things and couldn't watch TV because of all the commercials about toilet cleaners. They made me sick. Why had it been so easy to conceive before and now it was so difficult? I felt like a watched pot.

We then did an intrauterine insemination. I had read up on supplements that might help and took bee pollen and evening primrose oil and vitamin B along with my prenatal vitamins. I read the infertility chat rooms on the Internet. I kept telling myself that our baby would come when it was time, but my patience was thinning.

With all the testing and doctor visits, I began to grow tired of being so consumed with the process and decided to go back to work. I found a good job in my field and was scheduled to begin work on November 1, 2004. On October 20, 2004, we did our third IUI. Just before the procedure, my doctor told me that we would move on to injectable drugs if this did not work. By November 1, I was twelve days past ovulation and our most recent IUI and had not yet gotten my period. I was having normal PMS and had already started thinking about what our getting-pregnant plan would be for the following month. I was certain my period was on the way because I was retaining water and just felt awful.

But this month was a little different. I had gone for twenty-two whole days without a migraine. Those cyclical headaches were like clockwork, and I could always tell what was happening during the month (ovulation, period, etc.) when I had them.

I had to make some decisions about some upcoming meetings at work and decided to do an at-home pregnancy test a few days early. I was sure it would be negative, like all the others. It was positive. I was pregnant.

I was shocked, nervous, shaking, crying, happy, and elated. I could not believe our good luck that day.

At forty weeks and five days, just a few weeks past my thirty-sixth birthday, my beautiful, healthy baby boy Daniel was born.

When dealing with infertility you have good days and bad. During bad days, I would hate the moms and even grandmothers that I saw in public. I would foolishly judge them and think they were *happy people who never had a problem in the world—simply because they were pushing a baby stroller or carrying a baby papoose. In my eyes, they had it all. I was always reminding myself to be patient. Some days I would have to look the other way, not go to baby showers, family events, or even be around children. I had to keep telling myself that infertility is no one's fault, but sometimes nothing helped me with the pain. I would cry in private to get it out of my system. I felt so alone.*

In judging those other moms and families I couldn't have been more wrong. This journey to parenthood is a perilous one. It's full of obstacles and setbacks and hardships. When I was first pregnant with Daniel, the girl who did my facials had a thirty-eight-week stillbirth. Another friend had premature ovarian failure as a teenager and had to use donor eggs. My own sister and her husband found out that the only way they could possibly conceive was to try IVF. They did IVF two times and both failed. They are living child free for now. My good friend from work could not have children at all because of early menopause and endometriosis. She eventually adopted from Russia. Another work friend tried for years to conceive and lost her first IVF at six weeks. One of my new friends lost her second (and healthy) pregnancy at five months due to a clotting disorder that she was unaware of. The truth is, there are lots of us out there. We just need to tell our stories.

No one can tell you how far to pursue the path to having children. Some women need only a little push from Clomid, others are successful with one or two rounds of IUIs, others will opt to be more aggressive right out of the gate (asking their doctors for in vitro as a first choice), and still many other couples will eventually end up in a surrogacy arrangement or adopting. All of these are viable options, as is deciding that you've had enough. As Shelly says, her sister, Veronica, tried for several years to get pregnant, including several rounds of IVF. At some point she and her husband decided to stop trying, to accept not becoming parents, and to turn their attention to being involved with the children of their siblings and friends. My own IVF attempts did result in a positive pregnancy, but not without a lot of twists and turns in the road. But that's the subject of our next chapter.

Resources

RESOLVE: THE NATIONAL INFERTILITY ASSOCIATION
7910 Woodmont Avenue
Suite 1350
Bethesda, MD 20814
301-652-8585; 888-623-0744 (help line)
www.resolve.org

RESOLVE has been around since 1974. It was started by a patient, who, like me, felt passionately that people needed better information and the process needed to be demystified. It is a nonprofit with a mandate to "promote reproductive health and to ensure equal access to all family building options for men and women experiencing infertility or other reproductive disorders." Its mission "is to provide timely, compassionate support and information to people who are experiencing infertility and to increase awareness of infertility issues through public education and advocacy."

THE INTERNATIONAL COUNCIL ON INFERTILITY
INFORMATION DISSEMINATION

P.O. Box 6836

Arlington, VA 22206

703-379-9178

www.inciid.org

The InterNational Council on Infertility Information Dissemination (INCIID) provides a wealth of information on infertility and offers guidance to those considering adoption. Its website is a rich resource in itself.

THE ENDOMETRIOSIS ASSOCIATION

8585 North Seventy-sixth Place

Milwaukee, WI 53223

414-355-2200

www.endometriosisassn.org

The Endometriosis Association is an "independent self-help organization of women with endometriosis, doctors, and others interested in the disease." They can provide you with the latest information available on the treatments for endometriosis and steer you toward local resources.

POLYCYSTIC OVARIAN SYNDROME ASSOCIATION

P.O. Box 3403

Englewood, CO 80111

www.PCOSupport.org

"The Polycystic Ovarian Syndrome Association exists to provide comprehensive information, support, and advocacy for women and girls" with the condition known as Polycystic Ovarian Syndrome."

INTERNET HEALTH RESOURCES
www.ihr.com/infertility

The Internet Health Resources site provides extensive information about nearly everything related to infertility: IVF, infertility clinics, donor egg and surrogacy services (surrogate mothers), tubal reversal doctors, vasectomy reversal doctors, natural infertility treatments, male infertility services, sperm banks, pharmacies, infertility books and videotapes, sperm testing, infertility support, and the latest infertility drugs and medications.

CHAPTER 4

If at First You Don't Succeed: Our Adventures in IVF Land

When our troubles first began, I vowed to never to give up the faith, to continue to believe in our dream of eventually becoming parents, and to do whatever was asked of us to that end. So when Dr. Ben-Ozer suggested that we consider in vitro fertilization (IVF), I stifled my fears, insecurities, and self-doubts. After all, I reasoned, we were now fully onboard this scientifically enhanced baby-making spacecraft. Why stop now? I kept picturing my beautiful baby just a few more promising steps away and willed myself into an optimistic frame of mind.

It was this renewed hope about conceiving our child successfully that I took into our first meeting with Dr. Ben-Ozer and our first two attempts at IVF.

I have to admit, after our first few intrauterine inseminations (IUIs) failed, I was actually kind of relieved and excited. IVF seemed like a more promising procedure for us and a more aggressive alternative, which I was all over! I read up on the in vitro process and was more or less mentally prepared for the pain and torture to come. With IVF, you get put on a medication (in the form of shots every day for six weeks) to control your cycle and optimize ovulation. Then, at just the right time, they "harvest" (retrieve) all the available developing eggs from your ovaries and introduce them to your husband (or donor's) sperm, *outside* your body, in a laboratory Petri dish. Very romantic.

The eggs need to fertilize overnight, and over the course of a few days the best-looking dividing *embryos*—yes, plural—are implanted into your uterus in a procedure called "embryo transfer." From there on, it's supposed to be more or less a normal pregnancy. I was getting the picture that I'd be seeing a lot more of my doctors than I would anyone else for the foreseeable future.

By now, I was also determined that *aggressive* was going to be my new middle name. I wanted the newest, the untested, the one-in-a-million chance to succeed at becoming pregnant, and I really didn't care what we had to go through to get it. I love animals more than anything and am a spokesperson for the anti-fur campaign for People for the Ethical Treatment of Animals (PETA), but if you would have told me that I had to fly to Alaska and club a baby seal to get pregnant, I would have said, "Give me that club and when does my plane leave?"

I really do not remember much about the procedures that were discussed that first afternoon. I can't even remember who was actually present, so eager was I to begin this new phase of fertility treatments. All I remember is that there were lots of words and phrases, lots of "do this, do that," "a good chance of this or that," Lupron, shots, Clomid, more words, percentages, drug names, crazy feelings, multiple births. Did someone say multiple births? Yes, bring 'em on.

Oddly, I also have flashbacks about how people looked. Not who they were or what they said, just how they looked. Their expressions. Some, I could tell, really believed I would become pregnant. Others had doubt in their eyes. Isn't that funny? I could see their doubt. Still others had expressions that left me clueless, and I remember thinking, "Why are these people even here? If we aren't all on the same team, if we don't all believe wholeheartedly in my chances of becoming pregnant, in my dream of becoming a mother, well then, we need to regroup." But, for one of the very few times in my life, I didn't say anything.

Through all that talking—that whir of words, explaining, describing, detailing—my heart was screaming, "Impregnate me already! Now! Use all the eggs. Combine all the cocktails. Make me stand on my head and spit BBs from my mouth! I promise. I will do whatever you ask. Just please make me pregnant."

Getting Me Regulated

And so it was that we started in vitro.

Shots were once again a part of my life, and I became fanatical about receiving them at the exact same time every day, despite my doctors' reassurance that precision timing was not all that critical. This drove Guy crazy. He knew that we had some wiggle room with the timing, but of course in my mind he knew nothing—*nothing!*—of what was required to have this child. (It's so easy to become a martyr during this process. If that's your nature, you'll need to take extra care to tone it down.)

Taskmaster that I was, every night for six weeks (and then for six weeks at a time during our succeeding attempts), I made Guy deliver the goods at exactly 6:00 p.m., or else. We had to synchronize our whole lives and work schedules around being together at 6:00. Can you imagine how complicated that can make your life? Okay, it might not seem like a big deal, if your life is very orderly and you work a normal job. But Guy and I have never exactly been nine-to-fivers. Our schedules look like something out of a horror movie. Which made for some pretty hilarious rendezvous. Most of the time we tried to do the shots at home, but a couple of times we had no choice but to meet up on a freeway off-ramp or in a parking lot because I was on a job and the clock was ticking. I remember being at a Madonna concert at the Staples Center and having to sneak off to a secluded area so Guy could give me a quick stick in the butt.

Madonna may have gotten over the fact that I skipped out on her performance, but to this day I have not! When your whole life is so centered around having a child, it's easy to forget that the rest of the world does not stop for you. Oh God, I remember how resentful I used to feel that others could just go on with their lives (or their concert tours), as if nothing important were happening. As irrational as it may sound, bitter thoughts and feelings like that become imbedded in you, and they're very hard to shake even after you come down off the drugs.

Fortunately, I got used to the shots pretty quickly. I had dreaded them so much at the beginning, but they really don't hurt all that much. And because they're intramuscular injections (which means they go into muscle and not vein), you really can't mess them up too easily. But, meanwhile, I was carrying syringes in my purse at all times, and my arms, legs, and butt carried the tracks of a serious drug user. I was convinced that everyone thought I was becoming a junkie. Between the injections of fertility drugs and then the regular blood tests to check my various hormone levels, I felt as if I were a human pincushion. And if that weren't enough, the medication made me feel like I had perpetual PMS—not to mention the fifteen pounds I gained in just the first round. Not that any of that would have stopped us.

Ms. Egg, Meet Mr. Sperm

Bear in mind, we hadn't even started the treatments yet. This was just the preparation! The real fun was yet to come: what they call harvesting, or collecting, my eggs, which the doctors would then introduce to Guy's sperm in a friendly little Petri dish. Can you feel the joy? Just jump up on the table, Cindy, and let's see how many of those bad boys we can suck out of your vagina today!

Meanwhile, Guy was back to his old take-the-magazine-and-do-it-into-a-cup routine, which didn't exactly thrill him, either. I know, I'm probably scaring the heck out of those of you just getting ready for your first round of IVF, but the truth is, it *can* be a little scary and you should prepare yourself for that.

If it's your first time, you might be frightened if for no other reason than you just don't know what to expect or what's coming next. If you're on your second, third, or even fourth stab at this, then you might be afraid that you won't produce enough eggs this cycle or that the eggs you do produce won't be of high enough quality, and you'll be sent home to start the whole process all over again. Which is kind of like getting an F in history class. You knew the stuff, did the homework, and still didn't pass the test. Not good! To say nothing of the fear involved in lying flat on your back on a stainless-steel table, feet in the stirrups, legs wide open (a most vulnerable position anyway), and a five-horsepower vacuum cleaner coming straight at your little love nest.

Once we got through the retrieval part, the doctors took Guy's sperm and my eggs and mixed them up in that little Petri dish, in the hopes that they'd find each other and do their fertilizing thing.

Then came the wait. If you've been trying to get pregnant, you'll know what I mean when I say how excruciating it is to have to wait two weeks to see if you're pregnant. Just wait until you're expected to watch the whole process unfolding in a Petri dish! As if trying to get pregnant the old-fashioned way isn't hard enough, IVF takes the waiting game and just puts it right out there—in living color.

In many ways it's kind of amazing, the whole idea that they can even *do* this. But when it's *your* Petri dish everyone's watching, with *your* genetic material swimming around in it, well, it can be unbearable.

Next come the embryos. When you go the in vitro route, it's not unusual to have two, three, four, even eight embryos develop each cycle. The doctors then determine which ones are the "best," meaning the most symmetrically dividing and best developed ones—Dr. Ben-Ozer says they look like "a beautiful flower"—which have the best chance of success. Then they decide how many of those beauties should be implanted into your uterus via a very soft and not at all scary catheter.

Sperm Fact

In every healthy ejaculation of semen there are 40 to 600 million sperm. The average sperm cell can live within the female reproductive tract up to three days after ejaculation. And you need just *one* to get pregnant! How hard could *that* be?

Lots of times, the reproductive endocrinology and infertility (REI) specialist will encourage you to implant just a few embryos and freeze some for the next go-round. Guy and I, using our new, aggressive approach to baby making, wanted as many good embryos implanted in each round as possible. I can't say that Dr. Ben-Ozer always agreed with our choices. But we managed to find a middle ground each time.

After implantation, which takes only fifteen to twenty minutes (and sometimes requires ultrasound guidance), we had to just turn our lives back over to Mother Nature, who was supposed to help those little darlings develop and implant just as if we had conceived naturally and were expecting a normal pregnancy.

Which of course, we weren't. There is nothing normal about in vitro fertilization. Amazing, yes, but normal, no. Frankly, you have to ask yourself what *normal* even means, when more and more people have to turn to IVF to get and stay pregnant. Add to this the very real possibility of multiples with each attempt, and we're talking the outer edges of norm, people. And here's why. To maximize the chances that you will get and, more important, *stay* pregnant, doctors have to play the odds. They're not going to waste their time and your money implanting only one embryo, as good quality as that embryo may be. Unless you absolutely beg them (and even then I'm not sure you would find a doctor to agree), you will typically want to try up to six embryos each time.

Now that doesn't mean you'll end up with sextuplets, although there's always that chance when you play with Mother Nature. Usually, however, despite the implantation of multiple embryos, only the strongest will survive past the first few days, leaving you with a much more likely chance of having the one child you are planning for.

During IVF, and particularly just about this time in the process, you'll also start to hear all sorts of interesting clinical terms like *selective reduction*, which means exactly what you think it means. Aborting one or more of the fetuses you have just implanted. The truth is that sometimes it's medically necessary to remove one or more of the embryos because they look like they won't make it, and removing them early on is safest for all concerned, including the other, healthier embryos. You may also decide yourself to reduce your pregnancy because you simply can't fathom the thought (or the expense) of raising more than one at a time. On the other hand, selective reduction can also *raise* your risk of miscarrying the others, so it's a tough choice no matter who is making it. This is why I told you earlier to talk about these things with your partner and know where you each stand on these important issues.

Of course the doctor should discuss all this with you before actually performing the embryo transfer.

At any rate, now, while you are hot and heavy into the emotional and physical process of IVF, is just *not* the time to be thinking of this stuff for the very first time.

If multiple embryos survive past the first nine weeks (the first trimester), your doctor will then ask you what you want to do. Remember how I encouraged you to think about the possibili-

Nationally, overall pregnancy rates for a single in vitro fertilization cycle are 30 to 35 percent. Of those, 25 to 33 percent will be twins and fewer than 5 percent will be triplets.

ties and discuss them with your partner ahead of time? Well, here's one of those areas where doing your homework will really count. While it's true that you can't always anticipate how you'll feel when it's actually happening, and you'll probably still have some hard thinking to do, at least you'll have prepared yourselves. And that will give you a big jump on things. These decisions are difficult, but checking in with your heart ahead of time can really help.

Some women and men find themselves feeling suddenly very religious or spiritual at moments like these, as if a higher self were called to respond to the challenge of multiples. Frankly, I can't say I know what I would have done if I'd been pregnant with—or had to face the prospect of—more than two at a time. When our second pregnancy was twins, we didn't have anything to discuss. We were told we were having two, and we were thrilled. Stunned, amazed, shocked, even—but still thrilled at the prospect of bringing two new babies into our family. But more about that later.

I was put on bed rest for three days, which is pretty standard with IVF. I then had to wait twelve agonizingly long days to find out if our little adventures in the lab had actually resulted in making me pregnant. Despite the excellent preparation we were given, we just couldn't imagine it wouldn't work for us on the first try.

The day I went for my pregnancy test following that first procedure, I believed with all my heart that I was pregnant. When

> Try to remember: IVF doesn't always work on the first try.
> And if it doesn't, it's certainly not your fault.

the test came up negative not only was I heartbroken but I also became downright hostile. I questioned the nurse's qualifications to read the test results accurately, and I wouldn't let it go until she paged the doctor, who calmly but firmly repeated the words that I did not want to hear: "Cindy, you are not pregnant this month." Still unconvinced, and insisting that something was wrong with their stupid tests, I begged to please let me pee on the stick again. Knowing that was the only way to calm me, my doctor agreed to test me again, but of course the second test came up negative, too.

Hitting Bottom

Until that moment, the phrase *hitting rock bottom* had never meant much to me. But I suddenly had the full force of those three words choked up right at the base of my throat, and hard as I tried, I couldn't make them go away. I couldn't release them. Was it possible that I had come this far and was still going to end up babyless?

I went home that afternoon, got into bed, pulled the covers over my head, and cried for a week. I was sure I couldn't go through this anymore. Never again, not even one more time. The next month, though, we were back in the fertility clinic again. Dr. Ben-Ozer reviewed the first cycle with us as we all tried to learn what we would do differently next time to improve our odds. Guy in his room, me in mine. And if you think the second time around is easier, think again. Or at least it wasn't for me.

The stress on both of us was horrendous. I was resentful. I was angry. I wanted to hurt someone, and when Guy gave me the first shot in our second cycle of IVF, I wanted to pull the syringe out of his hand and stab him with it. How could he continue to inflict this pain and not give me a baby for my trouble? I wanted him to actually feel what it was like for me to be constantly poked and prodded. So the next time we went to the clinic, I actually asked for a set of practice shots not for me—but for him! Then every time I felt the least bit moody and sick of being stuck by this man who was supposed to love me, I would stick him right back! In hindsight, I think it was amazing that he even let me do this. But that's Guy for you.

By the end of the week, I was in hormone hell all over again, my feelings slaves to the emotional turmoil created by the drugs. I knew, of course, that I needed those hormones to stimulate my ovaries to produce on schedule, so that they, in turn, would (I hoped) produce more follicles, which would lead to more eggs. But they made me feel like a wreck. I had little control over my moods and, to a lesser degree, over my words or my actions. I would burst out crying hysterically or threaten to get in my car and just leave.

Once Guy even said to me, "But where will you go?" I didn't have a clue, but it pissed me off even more that he was asking. I felt like I was completely losing my mind, and I had no idea how in the world I was going to get it back.

I kept telling myself: "Cindy, this is normal. It's the hormones. You'll get past this," but I really felt like I never would. Sometimes it seemed like Guy and I and our lives together would remain out of control forever. Worse, I feared that we would struggle and struggle and still end up childless, and I simply couldn't accept that.

When Is Enough Enough?

We ended up trying assisted reproductive therapy (ART) three times without success. Three cycles of drugs and harvesting and implantation and bed rest and waiting, only to have to endure more bad news. It's difficult to keep any kind of perspective when you're in the middle of that kind of chaos. You just feel so out of control, both individually and as a team. There was little that Guy and I could do but follow our doctor's orders, and when that didn't work, there was no one to point a finger at, no one thing to zero in on, no one reason you could identify and say *"ahhh*, that's what went wrong," and then fix it.

So I took things out on Guy.

He was the one person who would not walk away from me, and here I was quite possibly *driving* him away. Just when we really needed to unite and stand strong in our love for each other, I seemed to be hell-bent on prying us apart.

> You just feel so out of control, both individually and as a team.

Thank God Guy could see through my facade. I count my lucky stars every day to have a partner who hung tough with me through *four* failed ART attempts—and then kept going.

It was almost impossible to remain optimistic about our chances of ever having the family we longed for. I felt tired, bruised, and fat; and I was sure that even our doctors were preparing us for the eventual throwing-in-the-towel ceremony. "Three IUIs and three IVF attempts is a substantial effort," our doctor told us. "You gave it a good shot. For reasons that no one seems to be able to figure out, the embryos that we've placed in your uterus just haven't taken. No one will fault you for wanting to give up. No one will judge. No one will say that you didn't try your best."

I was devastated. Guy said he would love me and be happy with whatever decision I came to. It was my body after all that was taking the hardest hits. He said he would understand if I felt enough was enough. But my heart said we couldn't give up. My heart said it was *our* decision to make. *Our* family. *Our* future. This wasn't a *me* decision. We started this journey as a team. It was no time to go solo. We needed to make this choice together. So we did.

We weighed the options as they were presented and decided to try just one more time before taking a different path. If this attempt failed, well then, we would more seriously pursue adoption. But we agreed that we had to try at least one more time.

Gamete Intrafallopian Transfer: The Winning Ticket

Guy and I entered the next phase of our infertility treatment with a renewed optimism and were even almost excited again at the prospect of a successful pregnancy. As we thought about our past failures, we really didn't have anything concrete to hang our optimism on, that was for sure. But Dr. Ben-Ozer had mentioned that a more aggressive procedure might help us—and remember, I was all about aggressive. That was my word. I just had this feeling in the pit of my stomach: *This time it was going to work!*

So off we went into our next appointment, refreshed and eager to learn the details that would make us winners in the baby game at last. Well, that's what I was thinking, at least. It turns out that the new aggressive procedure Dr. Ben-Ozer had hinted at was a combination of IVF and something called gamete intrafallopian transfer (GIFT), a procedure that would take IVF one step further by transferring the fertilized embryo directly into my fallopian tubes, which can provide the embryo with something it isn't getting in the Petri dish. Less risk, they said, that something could go awry before the fertilized embryo made it to its final destination.

I later learned that the reason we weren't told about GIFT (or zygote intrafallopian transfer, ZIFT) right away is that it is more costly and invasive and, for the majority of patients, it doesn't improve the odds of a successful outcome. For Guy and me it was a different story. GIFT could quite possibly help us, and we jumped at the chance, any chance, to increase the odds in our favor. The procedure, at least from my perspective, was not that much different. It was just IVF plus laparoscopy. The *magic* was in the mix, once the doctors gathered the ingredients. I was still going to have to lie on a sterile table, numb from the waist down, while they did their thing. I would still have to go home for three days of bed rest.

As the twelve days ticked by, however, I became more and more terrified. I just couldn't bear the possibility of another negative pregnancy test. Fear, doubt, and anxiety were all back in their usual places around my heart.

Confined to my bed, I thought about how I had done all that I could do. I had given everything I had—been all that I could be. Guy came in periodically to check on me. Often he found me crying. Whenever I had to pee, I would be afraid to stand up in case that was the extra second our child needed to arrive in its safe little haven inside my womb. I was even afraid to sneeze! Once, my cat jumped up on my stomach and I was sure that I had just lost the baby.

It's grueling enough waiting the twelve days, but wouldn't you know it, this time day twelve fell on October 1, my birthday. I knew this would either be the best birthday of my entire life—or the worst.

I was a total wreck. We went to the hospital in the afternoon, and I gave my blood, but I couldn't bring myself to stay for the results. I just couldn't. But just as we were hurriedly trying to exit the clinic, we heard screaming—the happy kind—coming from behind the nursing station. We turned back to see my doctor and the entire staff smiling and running to congratulate us.

"Cindy! Guy!! Wait!!" they yelled loud enough for the whole world to hear. "You're pregnant!! Congratulations!!"

I could hardly believe my ears. Happy thirty-sixth birthday to me! I have no words to tell you how that felt. We were over the infertility hump. We were going to be parents. We were *finally* going to be parents!

It was literally days before the impact of being pregnant actually hit us. For days after I went around practically singing, "Thank you, God. Thank you, world. Life is good."

Nine months later, I gave birth to our son, Nicholas Isaac Starkman (named after Guy's father). I can't say it was an entirely easy pregnancy. I spent much of it in and out of the hospital. On and off of bed rest. On special diets and directives. At one point, at about week twenty-four, I was misdiagnosed with a hernia that doctors thought had made me go into precontractions. I was even scheduled for hernia surgery and actually on the operating table, with several high-risk pregnancy doctors ready to monitor the baby through the procedure, when they discovered that a fibroid and not a hernia was causing all my problems. Then I had two months of solid bed rest in the high-risk pregnancy unit, followed by several more weeks of bed rest and monitoring at home—all in an effort to keep our son happy, healthy, and stationary in my belly—until that beautiful day in June when he arrived in all his glory to make us, *finally*, a family.

We were very blessed to be able to use GIFT with IVF. New developments in this field are happening all the time. I'm very excited about the less-invasive IVF work being done by the New Hope Fertility Center in New York and its founder Dr. John Zhang. Dr. Zhang has pioneered a "mini-IVF" procedure, which follows a woman's natural cycle and allows her (and her partner!) to avoid the discomfort of the shots as well as some of the side effects common in a traditional IVF. We probably would have gone with mini-IVF, had it been available to us. It's not only less invasive but can be less expensive, too.

Scientists in the field of reproductive medicine are constantly refining and improving the technologies and techniques. As of this writing, I know researchers are working on natural cycle

IVF (a no-drug IVF alternative), preimplantation genetic diagnosis (PGD), reduction of miscarriages, and improving embryo evaluation. All amazing possibilities for future infertility patients.

Of course, this is just our story. No two infertility stories follow exactly the same path. Some couples hit the jackpot and get pregnant with the first cycle of IVF. Other couples on the second, third, or fourth try. And some couples try and try and are still trying. This whole process will test you and your relationship in every possible way. To say nothing of your pocketbook, but I'm getting ahead of the story.

Our friends Daniel and Nancy are using IVF for different reasons from ours. I told you a little piece of their story in the last chapter, about how his male-factor infertility problems affected their marriage. Here's the rest of their story:

Nancy and Daniel: Things Were Pretty Traumatic for Him

Our diagnosis was clear from the beginning. Due to a long-term medical condition, my beloved husband, Daniel, has a very low sperm count (fewer than 1 million per milliliter, when a "low normal" count is 25 million). We knew when we married that we would probably need fertility treatments to have a baby, and we even had our very first IVF consultation during our engagement. That was ten years ago.

Since then, Daniel has been undergoing some drug therapies to try to increase his sperm count. So he knows what it is like to undergo daily injections of hormones! The treatments have been modestly successful, but the count is still very low. That means that we have to have intraceptoplasmic sperm injection (ICSI) the variant of IVF in which the embryologist injects just one sperm into each egg.

Today, three years later, we are still on our infertility journey. Our first IVF in November failed. The ups and downs were incredible! I produced seventeen eggs, and I was so excited, because in IVF more eggs usually spells more embryos and therefore more chances at success in the end. You can imagine our devastation when the clinic called, twenty-four hours after egg retrieval, to say that none of our seventeen eggs had fertilized. I cannot tell you how much that hurt, and it hurts just to remember it.

We felt that we were at the end, that we would never have a baby of our own. Well, the next day we got a call saying that two of the embryos had fertilized after all, albeit a day late. They transferred the two back into me, but two weeks later I lost them both. We were devastated again, just sick.

Although our first IVF attempt failed, we are about to start another IVF cycle, and we are much more hopeful. We have changed clinics, and the new clinic has a much better reputation and success rate than the old one. The big difference is that our insurance paid for the old clinic but won't pay for the new one. So, like lots of people, we are now about to spend a big chunk of savings. But it's worth it. I am hoping to add a success story later on, but for now I am just thinking positive.

One Day at a Time

There is absolutely no one right way to go on this infertility journey. Some couples will decide to adopt after trying unsuccessfully at home with no medical intervention. Others will persist and persist. I've met couples who tried for eight, nine, ten years before finally getting pregnant. And I just read about a couple who tried IVF numerous times and then more or less gave up—only to get pregnant the old-fashioned way.

Now, looking back with a perspective not available to me before, I often think Guy and I were lucky. Our first successful pregnancy took two years on our own, then three intrauterine insemination attempts, three in vitro fertilization attempts, and one in vitro plus GIFT procedure. That's an awful lot to put any body through—and any relationship—for sure, but it by no means sets a record.

And needless to say, none of this comes cheap. It is not at all unusual for infertile couples to spend tens of thousands of dollars on the making of just one baby. Of course, you can spend that on adoption, too. How far you will take this and what choices you make . . . well, only you will know what's right for you. But in the next chapter we'll look at the costs.

Resources

FERTILITY PLUS
www.fertilityplus.com

This site is for sharing information about infertility—patient to patient. It welcomes submissions of material about your own personal experiences. The site covers the issues, provides links to newsgroups and resources, and even has a section on infertility humor!

CONCEPTUAL OPTIONS
12780 Danielson Court
Suite B
Poway, CA 92064
858-748-4222
www.conceptualoptions.com

Conceptual Options is a full-service program that assists clients in coordinating all medical, travel, and legal "procedures" related to infertility and conception.

CHAPTER 5

How Much Is That Baby in the Window? Figuring Out Costs, Insurance, and What Is and Isn't Covered

You're probably getting the idea already. This getting pregnant business can get expensive. *Really* expensive. Of course, I don't know of a couple who didn't think it was worth absolutely every penny, once they ended up with the family they'd always dreamed of. But it's something you have to go into with your eyes wide open. It serves no one to be ignorant about a factor as important as money.

The naked truth is that a basic in vitro fertilization (IVF) procedure will set you back between $10,000 and $25,000 per attempt. Costs can vary, depending on the medical facility you choose, your insurance, and your doctor, but that's the ballpark. Given the fact that your first try may not result in a pregnancy, you can see how quickly you could find yourself in serious financial jeopardy. The cost of having a baby even under normal circumstances can be difficult to handle, but the costs of having a baby when you're infertile can be downright prohibitive.

Guy and I would have sold our souls to have a child and, in fact, had to perform some creative financing moves to get through our initial attempts, mainly because we were new to this game and clueless as to what was required. My friend James lost everything, including his marriage, in his baby journey. You probably know of a couple who had to take out a second mortgage, exhaust their saving account, dip into investments, or seek personal loans from friends and family to cover the huge expense of assisted reproduction. The message? Do your homework and figure out what's best for you and your partner.

I'm going to give you a list of pointers. I don't pretend it's exhaustive, but it's a start. Talk with your mate about how far you can stretch, find out how much equity you have in your home, see what kind of help you might be able to get from family, hold fund-raisers. The important thing is to know your financial reality.

1. Ask about the Success Rate of Any Clinic You Are Considering

According to the American Society of Reproductive Medicine (ASRM), the success rate of IVF is about 23 percent. As I

The Average Cost of IVF

The cost of a basic IVF procedure depends on the medical facility you choose, your insurance coverage, and your doctor, but you can expect to pay between $10,000 and $25,000 per attempt.

noted in the last chapter, reproductively healthy couples have about a 20 percent chance of success in any given month, so medically assisted pregnancy raises your chances only slightly. Dr. Ben-Ozer boasts an average success rate for IVF of about 50 percent at her clinic, but *not all clinics are alike*. You absolutely *must* do your homework and find a clinic that is reputable and has a good success rate. I cannot stress this to you enough.

2. Discuss How You're Going to Finance Your Treatment

Before you get started, you and your partner should be discussing how you are going to finance your infertility attempts and determining your options and your personal limits. The costs associated with the process we went through, for example, far exceeded even the basic (and very expensive) IVF, and you need to weigh the risks and rewards of such choices based on your own personal circumstances. The first consideration, of course, is your medical insurance.

3. Consider the Related Costs

There are any number of related costs, including lost income. If you're lucky enough to get pregnant, it may become necessary for you to stop working. A healthy pregnant woman can often work right up to delivery, if she so chooses. But your pregnancy may be deemed high risk or you may be put on bed rest, like I was, so you should factor in your loss of wages or salary. If you end up having multiples, the usual expense of starting a family will be increased accordingly, which is also important to take into account.

4. Know Your Insurance

Some of you will be lucky enough to have good health insurance that will cover at least part of your costs. But the reality is that many, if not most, insurance companies provide poor or no coverage for infertility treatment. They will often deny what they consider any extraordinary costs associated with infertility, and in some instances you will not be covered for anything more than the cost of delivery. If, once you get pregnant, your pregnancy is determined high risk, for instance, your insurance may deny coverage altogether for the costs associated with that, such as a long prebirth hospital stay. They'll cover your delivery perhaps, but nothing above and beyond what would be considered medically necessary for a typical pregnancy and birth. I have one friend, a lesbian, whose health insurance covered the costs of

Determining Your Insurance Coverage

For a personalized summary of your infertility insurance coverage, call Fertility LifeLines at 866-LETS-TRY (866-538-7879). This is a free and confidential educational resource provided by Serono, Inc. (a company that manufactures infertility medicines).

intrauterine inseminations (IUIs), but only if her doctor could document that her partner had very low sperm counts or no sperm. Well, thankfully, her doctor had a good sense of humor—and justice. She had no qualms at all about reporting to the insurer that the partner, indeed, had no sperm. No sperm at all.

It behooves you to know what *your* specific insurance plan will and will not cover. Every policy is different; even policies from the same insurer can differ from employer to employer. You simply have to know your own plan and thoroughly understand what it will pay for, what it excludes, and what if any restrictions it may impose. You should also be prepared to check and recheck with your insurer constantly to avoid horrible surprises.

5. What If You Have No Insurance?

You may not have any medical insurance at all. More and more of us are in this boat. If that's so, please don't lose faith. There is much being done legislatively right now to change that. There are also many organizations and charities coming forth to provide information and assistance for these very circumstances. One of the organizations that I am closely associated with (as their first Celebrity National Spokesperson) is RESOLVE, which I've mentioned throughout this book.

How does that help you as an individual trying to conceive? It's simply a matter of the squeaky wheel getting the grease. RESOLVE provides information and support and brings awareness to infertility issues through public education and advocacy; it is changing the way employers think. RESOLVE is making lawmakers stand up and be accountable for the myths and misconceptions about infertility that have in the past hindered coverage and assistance for those in need, and—perhaps most important— the group is there to provide us, you and me, with a one-stop infertility shop, if you will, where we can start the process of learning how to deal with our own personal infertility circumstances.

I have said many times in this book already and as often as I can in public, the biggest hurdle to my personal journey with infertility was the lack of readily available information and resources. Guy and I searched and searched only to come up with nothing much more than medical jargon that had no relationship to the specific infertility problems we were facing. RESOLVE is helping to change that, as are many other organizations and charities that have popped up in more recent years.

Michelle and Mike's story had a unique financial twist. At the point in their process when they ran out of money, they met an angel. Unfortunately, not everyone will have such luck. But in the middle of these grim financial realities, I thought it might be a helpful reminder that sometimes doors are not as firmly shut as you think.

Michelle and Mike: Sometimes There *Are* Angels

Our struggle with infertility goes back a few years. After several difficult years of not getting pregnant, we finally decided to go to a fertility specialist. After going through all the motions (the blood tests, the hysterosalpingographies [HSGs], surgery, etc.) we were told that we would never have children without the use of IVF. We were absolutely distraught. Not only was this something we were not prepared to hear but we knew the costs would be prohibitive and my

---

What's an HSG?

Hysterosalpingography (HSG), you may recall, is a procedure that involves injecting dye into the uterus, then X-raying continuously as the dye travels through the uterus and into the fallopian tubes to determine if they are blocked in any way. This procedure is also used to detect abnormalities in the shape of the cavity (septum, scar tissue), which can reduce implantation rates and increase miscarriage rates. Although often otherwise asymptomatic, such blockages or abnormalities can definitely make trouble if you're trying to get pregnant. There are surgical procedures available that can often remove such blockages. Because an HSG flushes the tubes, pregnancy rates also tend to improve for about six months after the procedure. Because this procedure can be a bit painful, your doctor may suggest that you take a nonsteroidal anti-inflammatory drug, such as ibuprofen, beforehand.

---

insurance wouldn't cover it. We figured there was no way we were ever going to have children of our own.

But we decided to go forward and figure out the money later. We went in for our first appointment and had the nurse teach us how to do everything. And then the day came to take my first shot. May 1, 2003. I'll never forget it. It was my fifth wedding anniversary. I took one look at that needle and cried my eyes out, like someone had just killed my best friend. Finally my husband was able to calm me down enough to shoot the needle in my butt. The protocol the doctor gave me at the time required me to take two needles in the butt, one in the arm, twice a day. It was awful.

After several days of taking the shots, and going in for ultrasound, it was time for my retrieval. I was so excited. Turns out I had a ton of eggs ready and waiting. When I came out of the anesthesia the doctor told me they had retrieved twenty-two eggs! He was so optimistic. We went home ecstatic. Then I got the call that seventeen eggs had fertilized and were "B to C" quality, which would mean a three-day transfer.

I went in all ready and full of optimism. I didn't even get into the transfer room when the doctor came to tell us that, over the course of the three days, the embryo quality had deteriorated. I just looked at him as if he were speaking a foreign language. But he sent me in to change anyway, and then came in and told me he was transferring five embryos but didn't feel optimistic.

More devastation. I cried the entire time. My husband just held my hand and tried to comfort me.

The doctor completed the procedure and came over and squeezed my hand and said, "Just try to stay positive." I knew right then and there that it was not going to work.

We went in for our checkup a week later. I had no symptoms,

nothing. They took my blood and sent me on my way. I then went in for my two-week pregnancy test and it was confirmed that I had not gotten pregnant.

I was so upset. My husband, the ultimate optimist, said not to worry. "We will have our child(ren) someday," he said. I must have cried for weeks. I went to work and fought with my coworkers. I had no desire to do anything. We did go back in July to do a frozen transfer [in which frozen embryos from previous harvests are implanted] but had the same results.

After about two or so weeks we decided we couldn't do this anymore. It was too costly—physically and emotionally—and I just wasn't sure I could handle any more heartache. We called the doctor and thanked him and told him we were done. He was totally silent, then said quietly that he thought we should really try again at some point. He was very optimistic about our chances of having a child, he said, it was just a matter of getting the right protocol together. He even said he'd give us a break on the cost.

I need to add here that I absolutely love my doctor. He really is the best.

We said we'd be in touch.

About three months later, the lady in billing called to ask, "Have you and your husband decided when you would like to start your next round of IVF?"

I told her, "We can't afford to start again. Thank you for checking in, though."

It was at that moment that I realized that good things do happen to good people. She said, "Mrs. Smaltz, someone has benefactored your next full round of IVF." I just about fell out of my chair.

I kept thinking: Who could have done this? Why did someone do this for us? I didn't know what to say. Was this some kind of joke?

Nope. In less than two weeks we were back in the doctor's office. I was having blood drawn every day for ten days, having my uterus examined—and then the good old shots. This time the doctor changed the protocol and ten out of the twenty eggs fertilized. They were all "A" quality. I was told I would have a five-day transfer this time. I was so happy!

I went into this IVF with a totally different attitude. I told myself during the entire process that I would get pregnant. We transferred two embryos. Everyone was so excited, even the doctor.

About a week later I started feeling so sick, but I didn't think anything of it. My stomach was really bloated. I couldn't sit, I couldn't eat, and I thought I was constipated so I started taking laxatives. Nothing helped.

What Is Hyperstimulation?

Ovarian hyperstimulation syndrome (OHSS) is, as the name suggests, an overstimulation of the ovaries as a result of assisted reproduction. It can be mild, moderate, or severe, causing everything from enlargement of the ovaries and related discomfort and fluid retention around the abdomen to nausea, vomiting, and shortness of breath to a life-threatening buildup of fluids around the body organs (heart, lungs, and kidneys) and a drop in blood fluid content. This condition requires urgent medical care and hospitalization to prevent liver failure, stroke, or heart damage. If you experience any of these symptoms after an IVF procedure, call your doctor immediately or, if symptoms are severe, call 911 or go to an emergency room.

I finally called the answering service and spoke to one of my doctor's partners. He said that it sounded like I was hyperstimulating. I didn't know what that meant, I just knew that I felt like crap. I woke up the next morning with the dry heaves. It was awful. But I didn't think in a million years I could be pregnant.

That Monday morning I went for my one-week blood work and explained to the nurse what was happening. She recommended that I take a pregnancy test right then and there. I was so nervous, I peed on the stick and there were immediately Two Lines! I just remember getting dizzy and needing to sit down.

I went in to see the doctor, and he suggested we take my blood just to be sure. About two hours later it was confirmed. I was pregnant.

A few weeks later, after four visits for ultrasound, I went in for my regularly scheduled appointment and found out I was having twins. I was deliriously happy. I called my husband and we just laughed. Sadly, at about twenty weeks I lost one of the babies, a little girl. She had trisomy 18 [a rare chromosomal disorder that can cause all sorts of severe birth defects] and we needed to terminate the pregnancy, as I was spontaneously miscarrying her. If we hadn't terminated, we would have lost our son.

Michelle and Mike had a healthy baby boy and are now getting ready to try again. It would not have been possible without the help of their anonymous angel. Of course, we won't all find such angels, and it just makes me crazy that the high cost of high-tech pregnancies makes it impossible for so many couples to have babies. I'm working to change this and encourage you to do the same.

Become an Infertility Activist

There are a lot of misconceptions out there about the cost of infertility coverage, and there's a lot of opposition to requiring it. Just check out an article by Bonnie Erbe that appeared in the *Pittsburgh Post-Gazette* on July 16, 2006. It offers a glimpse of some of the less-than-sympathetic views some people hold on the subject.

> **FORUM: MOTHERS OF INVENTION . . . ENOUGH**
> **"Older women who resort to in vitro fertilization treatments are being selfish and irresponsible," Bonnie Erbe says.**
>
> Finally, a mite of common sense in an ocean of insanity. A top British fertility doctor says "enough" to older women using in vitro fertilization (IVF) treatments to conceive. Dr. Sam Abdalla, medical director of a London infertility clinic, called for an end to IVF treatment for an ever-increasing number of women much over the age of 50.
>
> This after Patti Rashbrook, a British child psychiatrist (no less) gave birth at 62 to become that country's oldest woman to bear a child. Her husband is 60.
>
> Others even took Mrs. Rashbrook more sternly to task. The *Times* of London reports: "Josephine Quintavalle, founder of Comment on Reproductive Ethics," called Mrs. Rashbrook "selfish, irresponsible" and worse, adding she had "totally distorted nature. . . . What she has done is selfish, it is an example of putting her own wants ahead of those of the child. . . . I am sure the reaction from most of the populations to this is one of revulsion and distaste."
>
> Here, here! I've long thought the IVF/fertility industry and

the mania surrounding it's multibillion-dollar take ($4 billion per year in the United States alone) is driven more by vanity or desperation and adults' need to reproduce than it is by what's in the best interest of children or society. This is especially true in the Rashbrook case, where she already has three grown children ranging in age from 18 to 26 by a prior marriage.

Throughout the world, there are so many wonderful children in need of adoption. And with Earth's human population bubbling over the 6 million mark, and rising, there's hardly a shortage of people on the planet.

Americans are woefully uninformed about the hidden costs of IVF to society. A couple undergoing a single cycle (and most pregnancies require more than one) can expect to pay around $13,000 for treatments ranging from egg retrieval, sperm washing, medications, fertilization, incubation and embryo transfer. *Mother Jones* magazine reports: "Given all the failures and repeat attempts, the average amount spent per baby born through IVF in the United States is much higher: $100,000."

Luckily, few insurance companies cover IVF. But the fertility industry is certainly pushing for change. And once that happens, we'll all be sharing in the up-front costs. Even without coverage of IVF itself, everyone's health-insurance premiums are impacted by the after-effects.

That same article in *Mother Jones* contains some eye opening facts about a 2004 report by Johns Hopkins University, the American Academy of Pediatrics and the American Society for Reproductive Medicine. "It found that the biggest risk of IVF is the one we're all aware of anecdotally: multiple births. More than 32 percent of IVF births involve 'multiples' . . . compared to 3 percent in the general population. Nearly anything that can go wrong with a pregnancy goes wrong more often with 'higher order births.' . . . Babies born as twins are hospitalized twice as long as singletons, and over the first five years of life, their medical costs are three times as high. Babies born as triplets have a significantly greater number of cognitive delays. The average cost of a triplet birth exceeds $500,000."

Who pays? Every American with Health Insurance. And who pays even more dearly? The 40 million Americans who lack health insurance, because they can't afford premiums driven sky-high by what some would deem non-critical treatment (to wit, IVF).

Cindy Margolis—swimsuit model and actress—has recently become a spokeswoman for Resolve, the National Infertility Association, reports the *Oregonian*. This, after five attempts at IVF, a tough pregnancy that produced her now-4-year-old son and the birth of twin daughters to a surrogate last year.

With the intelligence and sensitivity befitting a swimsuit and *Playboy* model, she told the paper, "I'm a big PETA [People for the Ethical Treatment of Animals] supporter. But if you had told me I'd have to go to club a baby seal in Alaska to get my baby, I would've said, 'What time does my plane leave, and where is the club?' In the words of Bill O'Reilly: Cindy, please shut up.

Pretty nice, huh?

Note that Bonnie Erbe is a TV host and writes a column for Scripps Howard News Service. Her e-mail address is bonnieerbe@compuserve.com.

Your Homework

A couple of new homework assignments for you this week. *Talk* to each other and to your employer about your insurance coverage. If you don't have infertility treatment coverage as a part of your health plan then *ask* for it to be added. Many employers don't even realize that they need it—another awful effect of the taboo against talking about infertility. If your employer or insurance carrier balks, saying it would be too expensive, you can tell him or her this: According to a recent RESOLVE survey, 91 percent of employers who provide infertility coverage say they do not experience increased medical costs as a result. And yet only 20 percent of companies offer it. Tell others about the problem even if they don't balk! People need to know this.

Please check out the RESOLVE website (www.resolve.org) and get involved with the solution. If we don't help others, we cannot possibly hope to help ourselves. Your lawmakers need to know how you feel. They need to use their power to pressure insurance carriers to provide the infertility coverage we all deserve.

For insurance coverage specific to your state, visit RESOLVE's website at www.resolve.org and search for insurance coverage. Please familiarize yourself with the pending legislation and learn how you can help lawmakers understand the need to support this bill. Information from RESOLVE is online at www.resolve.org.

Write to Your Representatives

If you'd like to send a letter to your representatives about this issue, you can use the following letter, which is also available on the RESOLVE website.

Dear [Decision Maker],

I am writing to request that you sponsor legislation that would require insurance companies to provide coverage for infertility treatment, similar to H.R. 735, The Family Building Act, introduced by Representative Anthony Weiner.

Infertility is a medically recognized disease that affects men and women equally. Still, many insurance companies do not provide coverage for treatment to overcome this disease, but single out infertility for exclusion. I find this to be discriminatory. Well-managed insurance coverage will not place a large burden on insurance companies. Studies have shown that infertility coverage may actually reduce costs by limiting costly treatments that have low rates of success in treating the underlying problem.

In fact, a recent employer survey conducted by the consulting firm William M. Mercer found that 91 percent of respondents offering infertility treatment have not experienced an increase in their medical costs as a result of providing this coverage.

Insurers argue that bearing children is a lifestyle choice. In fact it is. But it is not a choice to have a disease that prevents a person from having the option to bear children. Insurers raise concerns about some treatments and the possibility of multiple births and the associated costs. Reproductive doctors are careful to help couples minimize the risks associated with multiple births. A study published in the *New England Journal of Medicine* (August 29, 2002) concludes that the incidence of multiple births is actually lower in states that have enacted an infertility insurance requirement than in states without coverage. Why? Because couples with insurance coverage are free to make purely medical decisions when pursuing some infertility treatments, as opposed to other couples who must also weigh financial considerations that often result in medical risk taking, multiple births, and a high rate of complications during and after pregnancy.

In 1998, the United States Supreme Court ruled that reproduction is a major life activity under the "Americans with Disabilities Act." This ruling demonstrates the importance of reproduction and the impact that infertility, in which the ability to reproduce is impaired, has on the lives of men and women.

Many affected by infertility do not feel comfortable speaking publicly about this very private struggle, but we represent all racial, religious, and ethnic groups as well as both sexes. We are neighbors, coworkers, friends, and relatives; and we just want to experience the joy of raising families without having to bankrupt ourselves in the process. Please support infertility coverage legislation and help fulfill the dreams of thousands of couples waiting for a family to love.

Sincerely,

[Your Name]
[Your Address]
[City, State ZIP code]

PART 2

Other Options for Growing a Family

Surrogacy, Gestational Surrogacy, Third-Party Donors, and Adoption

CHAPTER 6

She's Having My Baby: Choosing Surrogacy

Okay, after all that talk about money and social policy, let's get back to babies and how to make them! Just remember, this is all important stuff. Unfair insurance practices and lack of access to money and resources should never keep people from having kids, and it truly is up to each of us to do our part to see that we overcome these all-too-common obstacles.

But let me climb down from my soapbox and get back to discussing how to make your baby dreams come true.

Medically assisted pregnancy in its many forms—intrauterine insemination (IUI), in vitro fertilization (IVF), gamete intrafallopian transfer (GIFT)—is only one route open to you once you find yourself in the land of infertility. If you've tried some of these medical options, you may well be exhausted and depleted both emotionally and financially. Perhaps you're even feeling as though you were entirely defeated, but please don't give up hope. I know this is the easiest thing to do right now. Throw in the towel, tell yourself there is nothing else to try. But there are still a number of other viable options such as surrogacy, third-party (egg and/or sperm) donation, and the many types of adoption. As I so often say to people who need to know that it's worth it to keep going, *Believe in your dream to become a mother.* There's almost *always* a way.

Guy and I looked into both surrogacy and adoption at different points in our infertility journey. We ultimately chose surrogacy, so I'll start there.

With a Little Help from a Friend

First of all, what is surrogacy? Let me explain a bit about how it works. Surrogacy is the process by which another woman carries and gives birth to your baby for you, either with or without using your egg and sperm. This option is attractive to a lot of couples, as it was to me and Guy, because the baby is still biologically connected to at least one, if not both, of you.

The Cost of Surrogacy

The average agency surrogacy fee for a single, normal birth can be as high as $80,000. You can sometimes reduce the costs by seeking an independent surrogate, but in doing so you will have to weigh the associated risks. You should also be aware that the surrogate herself receives only a small percentage of that pot. In most instances, not more than 15 percent of the total cost goes to her.

It can also be one of the most expensive. Not music to our ears, for sure. The average agency surrogacy fee with a regular birth, no multiples or complications, can be as high as $80,000 or more. That may sound outrageous, but consider carefully what the benefits are, particularly if you find yourself in a similar situation to ours.

Our son, Nicholas, brought so much joy into our home and our family that we knew we wanted more children. Sure, there are nights you can't sleep. There's the general chaos and upheaval, at least for a while. But in exchange you get moments of joy and wonder you can't possibly describe. How can you not want more of that?

The thought of continuing down the IVF path after those last two tries, however, just did not seem like the right way to keep going. We knew the risks would continue to be high for me even if I finally did conceive again. Our doctors had warned us after Nicholas's birth that a future pregnancy would be difficult if not impossible. In my heart, I knew all that was true, but I was also determined to find a way to have another child. Our family simply had more love to give, and we wanted Nicholas to have siblings that he could grow up with. It would be worth it— whatever we had to do. Nicholas was proof of that. I know that plenty of couples have just one child and that can be the absolute right choice for them. For us, I felt that at least one more baby was in our future.

Fearful for my health, Guy was not enthusiastic about any further IVF attempts and had point-blank asked the doctor if my body could even withstand going through all that poking and medicating again, not to mention going through another pregnancy. She reassured him that I probably could weather another try or two, but she could not (would not) raise our hopes about the chances of another successful full-term pregnancy. She suggested that we think about surrogacy if his concern for me was too great.

As Dr. Ben-Ozer described the surrogacy process in more detail, I fully embraced the idea and found that even Guy was warming to it as a more acceptable option for us. We still had no way of knowing yet the full impact of the surrogacy process, but the knowledge that our baby could still be biologically ours was a wonderful plus. With this thought in mind, I began my research. I bought and downloaded every piece of literature on surrogacy that I could get my hands on.

Guy, once again, was having a harder time. For starters, seeing all that literature piling up on my bedside table did not exactly make his heart go all warm and fuzzy. I think knowing that I would undoubtedly take this challenge to the nth degree, as I did with everything in my life, scared him more than he was willing to admit. And on top of it all, I'm sure he was afraid that we would fail in the end, and that he would once again be in the position of having to console me (or our marriage) through another twelve months or more of heartache. He even said as much. But the more I read and the more I learned, the more I simply knew in my heart that this was the answer we had been looking for. We could have *our* baby without putting my body through any further trauma.

And so I had made up my mind. If Nicholas was going to have the brother or sister we wanted for him, surrogacy was how it was going to happen. Keep in mind that some women who don't have eggs of their own will need to use donor eggs and in some cases donor sperm as well. The eggs can be from the same woman who carries your baby, but they doesn't have to be. There are many options open to you in just this part of the process, so my advice to you at the onset is to spend some time gathering your information. It is never a wasted effort to learn as much as you can about the issues and options that face you.

Finding a Surrogacy Agency

Dr. Ben-Ozer recommended that we contact an agency that specializes in surrogacy, and I started looking around at our options. Several close friends and relatives—God bless them all—stood in line to offer their love, their support, and their wombs. But we decided to go the agency route because we knew we'd need their expertise this first time out.

We checked out the first couple of agencies on the list provided by our doctor and ended up choosing the largest one because we (meaning *me*, mostly) thought a larger agency would offer more than a smaller one. As we (*I*) later discovered, the size of the agency has absolutely nothing to do with how good it is or how good a fit it will be for you. But we were first-timers, and there was no one there to show us the way.

Guy and I also chose our agency because it seemed to work with a lot of local surrogates, which was really important to both of us. Common sense told us that having a local surrogate would mean it would be a lot easier for us to participate in the pregnancy—*our pregnancy*—not to mention attending doctor appointments and other necessary visits. But we were also concerned about our son, Nicholas. In a normal pregnancy, siblings watch a mother grow; they see and experience her pregnancy in routine ways on a daily basis that is just not possible when someone else is

> If this is your first time trying surrogacy, go with an agency.
> This is just too tricky a road to go alone.

carrying your child. The new sibling gradually becomes a family reality in that way, and for a child, the naturalness of that process is important for accepting the new baby once it arrives. Or so I reasoned. But, sigh, that wasn't how our story was to unfold. (Remember lesson one: You are *not* in control.)

If we had it to do over, we might have chosen a smaller agency, and we wouldn't have limited ourselves right out of the gate to using only local surrogates. In hindsight, I'd say you almost have to look at the agency relationship in the same way you do your surrogate. You should start with a list of the things that are important to you and your partner, and then be flexible. Maybe being local *is* important. Maybe having a good relationship with the staff or a connection with the person in charge of helping you find your perfect surrogate is most important to you. It's a matter of knowing what *your personal* expectations are. Not all of them will be met, of course. And they don't all need to be. But knowing your own baggage can help you seek out the right qualities in an agency as you shop around. Recommendations from others, reputations, good stats, and careful screening are all important things, but if your agency doesn't offer the type of resources and assistance that meet your expectations, then it's not the right match for you.

In our case, once we picked the agency and filled out the mountain of paperwork needed to get through just the first steps, we were assigned several people to work with us (and eventually our perfect surrogate). There are a lot of legal issues, so of course you are assigned experts to explain all that to you. There are also all the financial aspects that need to be addressed and discussed before you find your surrogate: How much will you pay her? What expenses will you be responsible for? When do your financial obligations end? We were also assigned a caseworker to oversee all of these things and to answer our questions and point us in the direction of answers as we went along. And, finally, we were assigned a counselor.

Besides handling the psychological testing that is part of the qualifying procedure, your counselor can be a wonderful partner in this process. In the long term, his or her job is to help foster the relationship between you and your surrogate. The counselor can help you bond. He or she can mediate feelings and expectations. A counselor can be a wonderful person to have in a relationship

A Checklist for Selecting an Agency

- Check out recommendations from your doctors and/or friends or relatives, if you're lucky enough to know someone with surrogacy experience.
- Know your preferences for the type of person you are seeking, so that you can be sure you pick an agency willing to work with you on the issues most important to you.
- Look for an agency that offers a complete list of surrogate services but is flexible.
- Ask to see their success statistics, and check out the information provided to you.
- Ask to speak to previous clients, if possible.
- Explore the range of psychological counseling services that are available.

that starts out with you putting your baby dreams into the hands of a complete stranger.

Choosing a Surrogate

Before you walk into your very first agency meeting, *spend some time thinking about your personal criteria* for the ideal surrogate. Don't assume that everyone's needs are the same or that it's up to the agency to tell you what you're looking for. They will, of course, and they're pretty darn good at it. But you need to be sure from the start that your surrogate is the type of person *you* want, with the very same expectations of this journey as you have.

So, what did *we* want in a surrogate? Perfection, of course! Do you think I was going to turn over my precious embryo to someone who wasn't perfect for us? But of course we had to find the perfect person, and she wasn't waiting around for us to come pick her like a piece of fruit from a tree. Never mind how impossible it is to even *imagine* someone else carrying your baby. As I thought about it, it became very clear to me that it was important that I be able to feel close to this woman. I wanted her to be a part of our family and for us to be a part of hers. I wanted to be able to live vicariously through her and her pregnancy with our child. I wanted to go to all her doctor visits, be present at every session of ultrasound—in short I wanted to experience "our" pregnancy from beginning to end. A tall order, to be sure.

Could we have set our sights a little lower? I don't think so. An intimate connection with our surrogate became *my* number one priority. We were turning over our precious cargo, and I wanted to be able to walk alongside her as she nurtured and carried it to its full term. That may not be important to you, and that's fine. Many women go into surrogacy on the other end of the spectrum, wanting little if any personal connection. That's okay, too. Remember, this is a *personal* journey. There are no right or wrong choices.

Pick Us, Pick Us! The All-Important Letter

One of the first things the agency required us to do was write a letter to our prospective surrogate, introducing ourselves and our family and then explaining our situation and what we were looking for in a surrogate. I can't emphasize enough how important it is to put time and care into this letter. After all, this person has to choose *you* from a pile of other prospects, and she'll be the one carrying your baby for nine months. You want her to have a pretty good idea of who you are so that you make the right match. You will also want to weed out any potentially bad or unsuccessful matches right from the start. No sense in wasting your time, the surrogate's, or the agency's. Develop your letter with as much straightforward honesty and detail about who you really are and what you want in a surrogate as you can. As an example, a surrogate who didn't really want the parents-to-be hovering for nine months would not have been a great team player for Guy and me.

I slaved over our letter for weeks. I went over it with friends and relatives and sought their input to help me paint an accurate picture of who Guy, Nicholas, and I were and why welcoming another child in our family was so important to us. This is your first and only chance of meeting your perfect match. Believe me, details matter. You want her to know everything about you and your family that could possibly make her choose you over the other prospective families who are just as deserving.

Don't worry about how long your letter is. The agency will encourage you to write as much as necessary about yourselves as you can—and I spared no details. This is the crucial first step. If you make it through this phase it's only because you took the time to provide your potential surrogate with enough information to help her learn who you are and why you need her help. It's all about The Letter, which is why I'm happy to share mine with you.

Dearest Surrogate Mother,

We hope this finds you happy and well. We wanted to take this moment to introduce ourselves to you and to thank you from the bottom of our hearts for reading our story and considering being our surrogate mother. You are truly an amazing woman, and we could never begin to tell you how much this means to us. We are so very excited to start our journey. We are looking forward to sharing this pregnancy together and having a wonderful fun-filled family future with you!

We are Cindy and Guy and ours is truly a story of love at first sight. On September 6, 1998, after meeting each other on a blind date (yes, we recommend blind dates to everyone, as you never know who you're gonna meet!) and being together for a year and a half, we married the person of our dreams.

We didn't waste any time in deciding to try to get pregnant. We wanted to start a family right away, and prayed we would conceive on our honeymoon. We would have been so thrilled if I had come back with morning sickness. But, unfortunately for us, that was just the beginning of month after frustrating month of getting our hopes up only to be sadly disappointed.

After two years of trying, our hopes of being able to conceive naturally were not high, and we decided to seek the advice of a fertility specialist. After we were given many tests (if there was a one in a million chance I had something, I wanted to be tested for it), we were told we had "unexplained infertility." As crazy as this sounds, we were hoping they would find something wrong so we could work on curing a specific problem. We were told it could take years for me to become pregnant naturally, and there was also the possibility that it would never happen.

Longing to be parents and now in our thirties, we decided to look into in vitro fertilization as it seemed like the best option for us. It was heartbreaking when our IVF didn't work on our first try. The dream of parenthood is not always the easiest road, and at times we lost faith. But we knew in our hearts that someday, all we would be put through would be so worth it.

After my fourth IVF procedure I finally got pregnant! We were so happy to be pregnant. It was truly amazing. Although I had a very hard pregnancy, being pregnant was a time of such anticipation, optimism, and dreaming—as well as fear, insecurity, and self-doubt—for us both. We had never been so scared or so happy!

I was in the high-risk pregnancy unit of the Tarzana Hospital at twenty-four weeks of pregnancy due to many complications that risked our baby's life, and I had to stay on bed rest until I delivered. On June 9, 2002, when our healthy, happy baby boy, Nicholas Isaac, was finally born, we weren't just relieved, we were the most joyous and the most grateful parents you might ever meet. He was indeed our little personal miracle—our very own glimpse of heaven wrapped up in a little blue receiving blanket.

He was beautiful! And becoming his parents that afternoon in June was the greatest achievement and most humbling experience Guy and I have ever known. We thank God everyday for our precious Nicholas, and as we watch him grow we realize all over again how truly blessed we are to have him in our lives. There are moments when I watch Guy and Nicholas play together that I think my heart will just burst, it is so full of love and happiness! When I hear him holler, "Mommy, come see" or "Mommy, come play," I sometimes have to stop the tears from welling up in my eyes, remembering a time not so long ago when I thought I would never hear anyone call me by that name.

As much as I thought we wanted a child, as wonderful as you can only imagine being a parent is, Guy and I have both learned that it is just so much more! There are nights you can't sleep, for sure. But in exchange you get moments you can't describe. Moments you can't imagine could ever be yours. Moments you just can't believe will ever come again! And then they do, the very next day when your little guy wakes you up with a great big "Good morning, Mommy and Daddy!"

Nicholas has changed our lives in so many wonderful ways. He has taught us that as much as we thought we knew, we know nothing! We learn new and wondrous things every day, just as he does. As happy as we thought we were, there is no limit to the happy moments ahead for our little family. As much as we thought we could love, we can love more!

We'd like to tell you a little bit about us as individuals and about our family. I will tell you about Guy first. Guy is a restaurateur who, along with his family, owns several great family-friendly restaurants in southern California. I joke that I married him for the food! He is thirty-four years old, a little over six feet tall, and weighs about 190 pounds. He has dark curly hair with brown eyes. He is a big sports fan, loves to play basketball, and cannot wait to take Nicholas to his first Lakers game. He is very funny and loves music (even though it's hard to get Guy up on the dance floor, I think he's a great dancer!), and one of his favorite things to do is have big barbecues in our backyard with family and friends.

Guy is a people person. He is very loyal. He is our family's rock. Sometimes I wish he was more emotional, but he's always there for me if I ever need someone to talk to or just someone to listen.

Guy is my very best friend. He is an incredible father and role model for Nicholas. The love he feels for his family is on display, every day, in his eyes and in his actions. His devotion to our family is marked by his gentle strength and guidance. There is nothing Guy wouldn't do for us. You hear people talk about how they would lay down their lives for you. Guy actually would. Without hesitation. He gives us an incredible feeling of always being safe and secure, which allows both Nicholas and me the freedom to continue to grow and explore as individuals.

He's a hard worker and a wonderful provider, and at the end of the day, no matter how hard that day may have been for him, he brings home love and laughter.

Now I'm going to turn things over to Guy . . .

Cindy is thirty-nine years old—five feet, seven inches, 128 pounds, blond hair, brown eyes—and has a smile that lights up a room. Cindy is a self-made Internet icon. She first took

the Internet world by storm with her innovative website offering everything from sisterly advice to e-commerce. In our
home life, she's basically a homebody who enjoys nothing more
than staying in with family and friends, hanging out in her
sweats, and going to a movie over attending a Hollywood
event.

One of her favorite things to do is to rent a big bouncer for
all the neighborhood children to play in. Many times I've
watched her climb in right behind all the kids, and I have to
wonder who's actually having more fun . . . her or the children! She loves kids; animals; and all the happy, silly, gooey,
simple things in life. Chocolate milk, mud pies, and messy little boys are always involved in what she might describe as a
"good day."

She also has a heart bigger than all the world and spends
as much time as possible doing charity work. She also assists to
further the cause of the numerous women's issues that she so
passionately believes in. She enjoys spending time with her
girlfriends and truly treasures her friendships.

Needless to say, she's a great mother to Nicholas. Always
by his side to give him support and confidence. Always thinking of what's best for him in even the smallest of decisions and
choices that we both have to make each day. Cindy's attention
to detail where our son is concerned is mind-boggling to me,
and yet it comes as natural to her as taking a breath. She is a
great help to me and has taught me a lot about being a father
by the example she sets as a mother.

Although my work takes me out of the house for most of
the day, she makes sure I don't miss any of Nicholas's important achievements no matter how minor. At the end of each

day, I either get a detailed accounting or an entertaining re-enactment—a show just for me, starring my two favorite people in the world: Cindy and Nicholas! Although she likes an organized house, she's really a slob at heart. But that's okay, as she always provides a home and a home life that I can't wait to return to each day. One full of laughter and love, hope and enjoyment. I appreciate her and love her and Nicholas more than words can express.

Cindy again:

The past two years of our lives have been amazing. The three of us have built a family stronger than we'd ever imagined it could be. We truly never thought life could hold this much happiness. But as much as we have and as grateful as we are for it all, we cannot help but long for another child to share all our love and happiness with. To be able to give Nicholas a little brother or sister to grow up with would be a true miracle. All you have to do is look at the smile on Nicholas's face to see how happy he is, how well he's taken care of, and how much he is loved. And after a few minutes, you'll also see how smart Nicholas is! He loves his family with all his heart and will make the best older brother. He is already so good with babies and loves his younger cousins with such vigor and careful consideration that we often watch in awe of his ability.

We both came from families with siblings, and we were so hoping not to have an only child. Guy has a younger brother, Jason, who is married and has two children (we are their godparents), and we see them often. I have a younger brother, Cory, who was recently married in our backyard and plans to start a family soon. My brother and mother live close by, and the family all get together on Sundays. Nicholas and his new brother or sister are lucky to have all four grandparents available, healthy, and looking forward to welcoming a new baby and you and *your* family to *our* family.

We live in the San Fernando Valley of Los Angeles, where I grew up (yes, it's true, I'm a Valley Girl!) in a beautiful, gated, family-friendly community, where we feel very safe and secure. Our neighborhood is filled with nice families, and we live in a cul-de-sac where children can ride their bikes and play without fear. Our house is fun-filled, with a playroom and a great backyard. We're big animal lovers and have two of the cutest cats you've ever seen! On Nicholas's next birthday we're going to get him a puppy!

Being blessed with Nicholas was the best day of our lives. Nicholas gave us the gift of love, warmth, joy, wonderment, and the satisfaction of becoming parents (and, of course, a little heartache). We never knew we were capable of feeling so deeply. That's why we know from the bottom of our hearts that we will be good parents to another little boy or girl.

We have a strong marriage and are building an even stronger family unit. The addition of a brother or sister for Nicholas, another son or a lovely daughter for us, can only make our family stronger and more complete. We will always be there for our children, to help them, to guide them, to laugh with them, and to cry with them when necessary. But most important, we will be there every day of their lives to love them with all our hearts.

Honestly, did we ever think our perfect family would be conceived via IVF and a surrogate mother? No, of course not. But that doesn't take away from the fact that it is still perfect.

Having a baby was a miracle. Being able to meet you is a blessing. You are an angel. In a selfish world, you are giving so much of yourself and to a family by giving them the precious gift of life. You are touching so many people's lives.

We look to having a wonderful family future with you that will include as much sharing as you feel comfortable with. We would very much like to be there with you for most of your appointments, but we will also understand if you only want us near for the big events! I remember how it is to be pregnant: Some days you absolutely love having your family all around you and involved; other days you're happiest with just a little bit of space for yourself! We truly want what *you* want!

We love children, so if you would prefer to go to your appointment some days and be treated to an afternoon of pampering (maybe a pregnancy massage and a nice nap!), we'll be there to make it happen and to babysit so you can have that time for yourself. On other days maybe just sending a cleaning person over or dinner for you and your family would be a greater help. We are in the food biz so all your cravings will be taken care of—we make the best Snickers cake!! Our point being, whatever your wishes or whatever the day may demand from you, we would very much want to help in any way we can. Our instinct would be to shower you with all the love and attention you so rightly deserve.

We'll be there for you without question. We have always felt that family built through love can be just as strong (and sometimes stronger) than family connected through bloodline alone. We have many special people in our lives with whom we've built extended family relationships through love. We hope to embrace you and your family in that wonderful extended circle in our very near future. All our thoughts and prayers are with you, and we so hope to meet you very soon.

Warmest wishes always,

Guy and Cindy

What to Include in Your Letter

As you write the letter to your prospective surrogate mom, be as precise as possible in explaining yourself and what you are looking for. Be as clear as you can. You want a full contact experience? You need to explain what *full contact* means to you. You'll be amazed at the many different interpretations of just those two words. To some people, that will mean being there for all the procedures, ultrasounds, and monthly doctor visits. For others, that can mean simply a weekly progress call and attendance at the birth. Also think about and be prepared to explain your feelings about selective reductions, terminating for specific circumstances (like Down's syndrome) and what those circumstances would be, how and what role your religious beliefs may play in this journey, also how important it is to you that your surrogate share those beliefs.

Your surrogacy bond can be a complex, satisfying, and lifelong relationship that extends throughout your entire circle of family and friends. It can also be a purely businesslike partnership that will end with the birth of your child.

To have a successful experience that meets your goals, you'll need to know in your own mind before you even start this journey where along that path of such extremes you and your partner would like to be.

Of course, there are no straight roads in this process. You can

> If I could offer you just one piece of advice, it would be this: Look into your heart and think deeply about what you want, put it out there, and then be willing to trust your instincts. This adventure may end up being far different from what you ever could have imagined. But it has to feel right to you.

be absolutely positive that you want to do things a certain way and then later find that you have to change course. When we started down this road, we were convinced that we needed to work with a surrogate who lived nearby. In the end, our perfect baby angel was a woman who lived almost 3,000 miles away in a city and state that I had never even visited. And, despite that, our family shared an amazingly intimate and personally involved pregnancy. For sure it took a little more effort on everyone's part and a lot more traveling, but finding the perfect person far outweighed the inconveniences of her not living near us. And I don't want any of you making the same mistake I did, thinking that wasn't possible.

Matchmaker, Matchmaker, Make Us a Match

Once Guy and I finished our plea to pick us—and let's face it, that's exactly what you're really doing here—we turned the letter over to our caseworker and began the long wait. She took our letter, placed it in our file along with all the other paperwork and interviews that had already been completed, and scheduled an internal meeting with our team of agency staff to begin the match process.

We waited for weeks and weeks, which turned into long, agonizing months. Our hopes for a quick match waned. We were in routine contact with the agency, so we knew they were working diligently to find us a match. But as the days continued to roll by, it seemed more unlikely all the time. Until finally, near the end of the fourth month, we got a call to come in for a chat. They had found a potential match, one that *they* felt would be perfect, but they wanted to caution us up front: She didn't actually meet all of our critical criteria as outlined. That caveat gave us some pause, but we agreed to meet the following afternoon.

Meeting Shannon

My fears and doubts about introducing a stranger into our little family were quickly dispelled in my very first conversation with our surrogate. This call, too, came on my birthday, which to me was a good sign. As it turned out, two for two. I got my first and only positive pregnancy test on my thirty-sixth birthday and now I was meeting my first potential surrogate three birthdays later. Initially our counselor set up a conference call to introduce us and to start the process of building a relationship that could foster trust across nearly 3,000 miles. I was anxious that she like me. Worried that she wouldn't. And worried even more that somehow she might disapprove of our lifestyle or even my career as a model and actress. I later learned that Shannon herself had some of these very same concerns.

But we both worried unnecessarily. Shannon and I bonded almost immediately. Conversation was easy and flowed quite naturally, to both our surprise. We ended that first call with me asking her to go to my website, read a little more about who I was and if none of that bothered her, to call me right back. It was an agonizing twenty minutes while I waited, but when that phone rang from Minnesota for a second time that afternoon, I knew we had found our match. And on the first try!

Once we met her and her family, the relationship was easy, the bond forever, and the distance not even a consideration. So please, take the time to seek out the right surrogate for your situation and try not to limit yourself unnecessarily with preconceived ideas about what's important. Research your options, decide on your personal needs and bottom lines, and then remain open and flexible as you begin. Especially if this is your first surrogacy. There is so much to learn about each other. So many things you won't even know to ask.

Early on, Shannon came to Los Angeles to meet with my family, interview with our doctors and agency team, and to allow us both a little time together before the procedures actually started. When it was finally time to transfer the embryos, she returned for the procedure and for the three days of required bed rest. We spent that time together talking to her belly, encouraging our newest family member to settle in and begin to grow.

She returned home to her own family later that same week, and we both waited anxiously for news of a viable pregnancy. The day the news finally came and we learned that she would be carrying our twin baby girls was also the day of Guy's mother's funeral. Caroline had been praying for us just days before her death. Praying that Shannon would be pregnant and that yet another grandchild would bless our family. I felt like getting the news on that day was Caroline's way of putting joy and a loving touch on an otherwise very sad day for all of us. Shannon, Guy, and I were so very excited that we immediately planned a trip to Minnesota, so that we could meet Shannon's husband, children, and parents.

As our pregnancy progressed Guy and I made routine visits to Minneapolis to visit Shannon and her family and to attend as many of her doctor visits as we could. Sometimes I would go alone, sometimes we'd go together and take Nicholas along with us. When the girls' birthday finally arrived, an emergency C-section kept us from being all together for the wondrous event. But just a few hours after their birth (an eternity at the time!), Nicholas, Guy, and I were in those lovely blue hospital gowns, finally and amazingly welcoming our two new daughters into our family at last. Sierra Jean Karyn Starkman (named after my grandmother and mother) and Sabrina Caroline Shannon Starkman (named in honor of Guy's mother and as a lifelong reminder of our angel surrogate Shannon, who will always be a part of our family and our lives).

Surrogacy ended up being one of the greatest experiences of our life. Our beautiful surrogate Shannon and her family (Todd, Michael, and Madeline) were sent from heaven and brought with them the precious gift of two beautiful baby daughters for us— Sierra and Sabrina—to call our very own. When we first contemplated this route, we never in our wildest dreams would have imagined such a wonderful ending to our infertility journey. Having Nicholas was a miracle. Receiving two more such miracles is a blessing for our family beyond what words could convey. We feel so very blessed that our struggle to have children—one of the most difficult times in our lives—has ended so happily and so completely.

Angela and Joe had a different experience with a surrogate, and their own quite miraculous ending. You may want to go get a box of tissues right now and keep it close by as you read their story.

Angela and Joe: Be Careful What You Wish For!

Last year, we had just completed my sixth IVF and also had a friend (as our surrogate) do transfers at the same time. Mine did not take (I have unexplained infertility), but by a miracle, one embryo did implant with our surrogate, and we were so excited. We were so grateful to our surrogate for offering us such a wonderful gift and the chance to actually become parents. Our dream looked like it was finally coming true.

We had our surrogate move in with us so that we could help her with her son and await the birth of our baby boy. But in October, at twenty-four weeks, she called us in the middle of the night to come upstairs, and I knew immediately it was going to be bad. Really bad.

We rushed her to the hospital. It turns out she had preterm premature rupture of the membranes. After five long days, the doctors confirmed that there was zero amniotic fluid, and our surrogate was starting to bleed because the [ruptured membranes caused an] infection [that] was attacking the placenta. They had to induce labor, and our firstborn son was born alive after a thirteen-hour labor, but he died in our arms a few hours later. Both my husband, Joe, and my family stayed all night, and we were able to have Giovanni baptized. Then we just rocked him to sleep and told him how much we loved him and how happy we were to be his parents. We buried him a few days later and buried a part of ourselves with him.

All three of my sisters and two of our friends then offered to carry a baby for us. We went to our doctor and asked him who was our best candidate, knowing full well how fortunate we were to have a choice and such supportive family and friends. It turned out to be my youngest sister, Sara. She had just had her second child when she started taking the medications (Lupron, estrogen tablets, and progesterone injections) for surrogacy. Fortunately we had two frozen embryos left from the first round, so we did the transfer in April, and things looked good. We did have a positive human chorionic gonadotropin (hCG), but the numbers started to decrease, and unfortunately it did not work. We knew that we were running out of options, and our hopes of becoming parents to a biological child were fading.

We agreed we would try one more fresh cycle, and my sister was willing to try again. Because I had nothing to lose, we did our ninth IVF at the end of May. We transferred two embryos to my sister, Sara, and two to me. Now we just had to wait those two agonizing weeks to see if it worked—the hardest two weeks, because we knew this would be our last time.

Twelve days later our doctor's office called with the news of our miracle. My sister is pregnant with our twins, and by a miracle I am actually pregnant with one baby, so now we are expecting triplets!!! In a few days we will be thirteen weeks and praying every day that all the babies are healthy and we have full-term, uncomplicated deliveries.

Angela and Joe's story just goes to show that you can't predict outcomes in this crazy infertility game. What strikes me as so lucky is that Angela's friend was able to move in with them during her surrogacy attempt, and then that her sister, Sara, was close by as well. Of course, I'm sure none of them would have guessed they'd be having three! The point is, they had to be flexible, willing to change plans when Plan A didn't work out. You'll probably surprise yourself at how strong you can be when you need to be.

A Surrogate's Perspective

We've all heard and read tales of horror about adoption and surrogacy. Sometimes it seems that's the only story you hear. The woman who sounds good on the phone and gladly takes your money, never to be heard from again; the surrogate who decides near the end of her pregnancy or after the birth that she won't give up the child; the crooked agencies that take your money; the attorneys who don't dot the *i*'s or cross the *t*'s and end up complicating the legalities of such an arrangement. Of course things like that do happen. It's a crazy world and there are, unfortunately, some mean and troubled people who will take advantage of those in vulnerable situations like ours. But most surrogates are really incredible, giving, honest women. In fact, you have to wonder what would drive a person, a perfect stranger at the start, to want to give so much of herself to a family like ours. To help you understand, I asked my own surrogate to share her perspective on the experience. Here's Shannon:

The headline read "The most precious gift: Minnesota mom delivers twins for Hollywood couple." Reading those words a few days after delivering twin girls to Cindy and Guy made my heart swell with pride. Here I was, at the end of my journey (or was it really just at the beginning of the next phase of a relationship?), which just a little over a year before did not even exist. How was it that a quiet, somewhat private wife and mother from Minnesota would end up in the media spotlight, alongside an outgoing, well-known couple from the heart of L.A. and the celebrity scene? This is a story that some would say could be written only in a Hollywood script. It is the story of heartbreak and joy, nervousness to familiarity, love and friendship, honesty and trust. Two families thousands of miles apart from each other, strangers, matched together, ready to start a journey with a single goal in mind: to make a baby.

Why, some would ask me, did you decide to become a surrogate mother? I really don't have a definitive answer. I can start by saying that I really enjoy the feeling of being pregnant. I love to nurture the precious life inside me and be the caretaker for the little being who is dependent on me for nine months. Surrogacy goes along with the type of person that I am. I like to help others and give of myself.

I look at my two beautiful children, the ultimate blessing, and I cannot imagine my life without them. Some calling inside me, or maybe from a higher power, told me that this was the path I should choose. Something inside my very heart says that I must go out and help other couples experience the same blessings of children that I am fortunate enough to experience every day. Something deep within me cries out to help those couples who have little hope of having children, except for the hope that I may provide them. Truth-fully, it's as much a need inside of me as it is a need that I am fulfilling for others.

Working closely with an agency, I was presented with a list of couples who were looking for their surro-angels. How could I choose which one I would help, when there were so many couples who desperately wanted children? Well, that decision ended up being an easy one, when I received a phone call from the agency that said Cindy and Guy wanted to work with me. I had read their surrogacy letter and immediately felt a kinship despite the obvious differences. These people needed me. I could feel their desperation, *their sincerity and warmth. A phone conversation was planned for the next day, and boy, was I nervous! But Cindy was so easy to talk to, and there was the instant connection that I was so hoping would be there.*

Thus began a special friendship, a whirlwind romance of sorts. Everyone getting to know one another, all the while a silent clock kept tick, tick, ticking in the background. It was time to get down to the business of making a baby, and after four unsuccessful attempts at a match and almost a year of searching for a couple to help, I was as anxious to get started as they were.

Within two months of meeting Cindy and Guy for the first time, I was out in California, ready to have their precious embryos inside me. We transferred a total of three eggs, and oh, how I prayed that at least one of them would settle in and stick around for a whole nine months.

Two weeks later, three days before my official blood test at the obstetrician, I broke all the rules and decided to secretly take a home pregnancy test. I knew I shouldn't do it. For a lot of good reasons, they tell you not to. But I just had to know. Were all the symptoms I had been feeling just a figment of my imagination?

Well, within thirty seconds I had my answer. No figments! I was pregnant! Yes!! I couldn't believe it! I was so happy! Someone had decided to find a home inside of me—a new life and a new family was making its first start. I was elated.

I couldn't wait to call Cindy and Guy, and they were, needless to say, also very excited. Cindy kept asking me if I was really sure, so I took another test while I was on the phone. Guy was happy, but he really wanted to wait for the official word from the doctor three days from then. I think they were both in shock that it had worked the first time. Within a week, we all knew that something even more extraordinary was going on, as my beta hCG numbers continued to climb quickly.

At six weeks, it was time for the first ultrasound. I remember being shocked and then completely overjoyed. Twins! Both looked great, and I was able to see their little hearts fluttering away. Driving home, I was just bursting at the seams. Cindy and Guy called for the results, and I got teary eyed as I hollered into the phone, "Twins!" Cindy kept saying, "Oh my God! Oh my God!" This intense emotion that all of us were sharing made it perfectly clear to me that becoming a surrogate was the right thing to do.

Throughout the pregnancy, our relationship continued to grow. Our families became enmeshed with one another, and even though we were far apart, it always felt as if we were together. I told everyone who would listen about our story. I was so proud to be helping create a family.

I never felt like Cindy was a celebrity; she was just my close friend, and we were sharing an awesome experience. After the delivery of the girls, I remember walking into the nursery one evening to see Cindy and Guy holding their babies. I was looking at a family that would not have been complete if I hadn't offered myself as a guardian and a carrier. It is hard to explain the feelings of pride and love, and also a bit of sadness at the thought that the babies did not need me anymore. I did my job, and they were where they belonged, in the arms of their mommy and daddy.

Big brother Nicholas was so sweet and gentle with his baby sisters. My family went into the nursery to see the babies, too, and to say good-bye. The circle that had started eleven months earlier was now complete.

How was I going to feel when this family that I had shared so much with left Minnesota and me for the last time? This was the scary part, and more than one person had expressed concern over how we would all handle this ending. For me, there was never any doubt that I would and could disconnect.

From the start they were Cindy and Guy's children. I was never more than their hand-picked glorified babysitter, and I was so grateful for that. It was enough. No, it was more than enough for me to have this beautiful experience. To provide the most precious gift of life to a family so deserving and with so much love in their hearts to give these very special little girls. I felt no sadness for the babies and maybe only a little for the part of the journey that was now over for me.

But I had no fear that the special relationship that all of us shared would come to an end with the departure of the babies. I have been one of the fortunate surrogates whose intended parents wanted to remain in touch and continue the relationship. Did the relationship change? Well, yes, a little. As I had hoped it would. Life got back to normal for both families, or as normal as a household can be with three small children. I went back to all my prepregnancy activities, and my focus, which had been on the pregnancy, returned to my own husband and kids.

Phone calls and e-mails have tapered off as time has gone on, because busy lives for both families seem to take up so much time. But do I doubt for one second that Cindy and Guy aren't grateful to me? No way! Nothing in any of our lives could ever change the relationship that we created while completing their family.

Does my story end here? Well, no, not exactly. I had so much fun and found so much purpose in my first journey with Cindy and Guy, that I have decided to help another couple. I am currently getting ready to start my second surrogacy journey, and all the feelings of hope and anticipation have returned. There are already differences in the relationship that we are forming, but in my opinion that is a good thing. I want a different journey from the one that Cindy and I shared. I can only pray that this journey is as fulfilling and blessed as the previous one.

Some people say that I am an angel for helping couples the way I do, but I don't look at it that way. I know deep in my heart that this was the path I was meant to choose at this point in my life. And now the circle starts again, ready to be completed with the sound of another newborn's first cry.

Shannon

Surrogacy is one of those amazing experiences that you don't necessarily set out to choose but that can expand and enrich your life in ways you could never have imagined. We had—and continue to have—an incredible experience with Shannon. She enabled us to have two more children who are biologically connected to us both. We continue to share moments and holidays of extended family connection. Guy and I will never forget the love she shared that enabled us to complete our family, and one day we hope to share the details of this long journey with Sierra and Sabrina as well.

We know things don't always go this well. But surrogacy provides you an opportunity to have a child that is genetically yours and your partner's (or to at least one of yours), and you very often do end up connecting with an incredible woman and her family and learning the true meaning of the word *generosity*.

Plus you get the extra gift of teaching your children, and yourselves, that often it *does* take a village to raise a child, right from the very start.

Resources

What follows is a list of reputable agencies both large and small, none of which you should choose without doing your own homework. I'm including the contact information for the Center for Surrogate Parenting (CSP), which is the agency Guy and I worked with. It is very reputable, but I am not endorsing it above others. Other agencies might have met our needs quite well had we been less rigid in our thinking.

SURROGATE MOMS ONLINE
www.surromomsonline.com

This site "provides information and support to people interested in pursuing a surrogacy or egg/sperm donor arrangement." It is completely independent and "not associated with any professionals in the field of surrogacy, adoption, egg donation, or sperm donation."

ADOPTION & ASSISTED REPRODUCTION LAW OFFICES OF DIANE MICHELSEN
Family Formation
3190 Old Tunnel Road
Lafayette, CA 94549

925-945-1880

www.familyformation.com

These folks have been doing surrogacy work for more than twenty years and are nationally recognized in the field. This firm also handles legal matters concerning adoption and assisted reproduction.

EVERYTHING SURROGACY

www.everythingsurrogacy.com

This site has an extensive surrogacy directory. It is privately owned and operated "for the purpose of promoting safety in the surrogacy community through education."

ALL ABOUT SURROGACY

www.allaboutsurrogacy.com

This is another online resource for surrogate mothers, intended parents, and egg donors. As its mission statement says, its intention is to provide the community "with a wide range of views about being a surrogate mom, an egg donor and all aspects of the surrogacy process."

CENTER FOR SURROGATE PARENTING, INC.

West Coast Office

15821 Ventura Boulevard

Suite 675

Encino, CA 91346

818-788-8288

East Coast Office
9 State Circle
Suite 302
Annapolis, MD 21401
410-990-9860
www.creatingfamilies.com

This is the agency that Guy and I used.

CHAPTER 7

Going Shopping: Egg and Sperm Donation

Sperm banks and egg donor centers are two other options to explore when medically assisted pregnancy isn't working. In fact, if you are determined to retain a biological connection to your child and you've discovered that either your husband's sperm or your eggs are giving you trouble, sperm or egg donation is often the *only* viable alternative.

Just in the last ten years alone we've seen an explosion in the numbers of gay men and lesbians forming their own families in this manner. In fact Guy and I have more than a handful of close personal friends who have or are presently in the process of forming families with the help of donors. My cousin Julie and her partner had a really wonderful plan. They used the same sperm donor, and each of them had a baby using their own egg and his sperm. The children are biologically connected to each other (as half siblings on the donor's side) and each partner had the experience of carrying and delivering a baby. A very well thought out plan, if you ask me.

I know another gay couple, Chris and Jim, who also used a donor—this time for the eggs. They sought out the services of a traditional surrogate, a woman who would both donate her eggs and carry the baby for them via in vitro fertilization (IVF). Each of them provided sperm to produce the embryos but were never told—and didn't want to be told—which sperm actually got the surrogate pregnant. They froze the unused embryos, and three years later found another surrogate to complete their family of four.

Plenty of couples are now pursuing this route. Some estimates show that as many as 30,000 to 50,000 American children a year are born from donor sperm, but of course, no one knows for sure—and for good reason. With donor-assisted conception, it's often possible to remove the one obstacle, either the egg or the sperm, that's been making it hard for you to get or stay pregnant and still have a baby that carries the genes of at least one of you. And that's just an example of how many ways you can choose to make a family! As I've said so many times before, *your baby dreams can come true!* Just sometimes, you have to be willing to think and explore outside of the box.

Sperm Banks

If your husband's sperm is the source of your infertility issues (and there are many reasons that this might be the case, from low to no sperm counts to motility problems to medical problems with the seminal fluid), and intracytoplasmic sperm injection (ICSI) didn't help, a sperm bank might be a good option. In fact, if your situation allows it—and only your doctor can help you decide—you may be able to "bank" your husband's sperm, use it after it has been made ready in the lab, and then freeze some of it for later use.

Of course, sperm banks also provide sperm for women who otherwise don't have access to a ready source, including single moms by choice, lesbian moms, and women whose husbands are unable to produce healthy sperm.

Again, I can't stress enough that you must do your homework. There are many, many reputable sperm banks out there, but there are clinics with problems as well. As for all your options, do not rely on sketchy information or unsubstantiated recommendations. Check everything out yourself and be satisfied, confident, and comfortable with the people and the clinics you choose to deal with. Their policies will vary widely, and you want to make sure the policies of the sperm bank you work with are compatible with your own values and desires.

For example, some sperm banks provide baby photos of their donors. Some even provide video. Some work only with donors who are willing to be known to the child once she or he hits eighteen (or sooner), whereas others do not have such policies. Some have a limit of ten families per donor, others have a higher limit; and of those, only some will facilitate the process of getting to know those other families, should you so choose. These are all factors you will want to weigh carefully as you make a decision about what's right for you.

Some offer material written in the donor's own hand. Most offer short profiles of their donors online, with more in-depth donor profiles available for a fee. You wouldn't believe what you can find out about these guys in advance. Not only hair color, eye color, weight, height, and all that but also their favorite foods, colors, hobbies, professions, self-assessments of their own temperaments, and often a brief explanation of why they decided to donate their sperm (and their answers will vary widely—from "I needed the money" to much more from-the-heart explanations). I have one friend whose mother, after hearing what she knew about her donor, told her, "Wow, you know a lot more about this fellow than I knew about your father before we started having kids!"

Most sperm banks ship their sperm all over the country (using FedEx and dry ice), so don't worry about picking one nearby. Choosing locally can be a great convenience and save you a little money in shipping costs, but some women actually prefer to use a sperm bank in another state or region, for their family's privacy and also so that future related children have less likelihood of meeting up accidentally.

About the money, by the way: Sperm donors don't earn all that much—up to a few hundred dollars per donation. Of course, their "work" isn't all that tough, but they do usually have to make a commitment to donate for at least a year, so it's not a good gig for flakes. They usually make a deposit about once a week. It's just not worth the clinic's time and expense to run a donor through the necessary tests and paperwork if he's not going to stick around at least that long.

To ensure that donated sperm is free of sexually transmitted diseases (STDs) sperm banks routinely quarantine each deposit of sperm for six months and then recheck the donor. If he's STD-free, they then release the six-month-old deposit.

Usually you'll have the opportunity to review the donor's

own physical and mental health history as well as the histories of his mother, father, siblings, and grandparents.

These banks also vary widely in which genetically inheritable diseases they screen for. For instance, many will test only their Jewish donors for Tay-Sachs disease, because it is most prevalent in the Ashkenazi (of eastern European descent) Jewish population. But Tay-Sachs does occur in other parts of the world, and if you yourself are a Tay-Sachs carrier, you will probably want to work with a sperm bank that tests *all* its donors for this rare disease. This is just one example.

Some clinics will allow you to "prepurchase" several months' worth of a donor's sperm, to be sure you don't run out before you've had success. And if you want more kids, you may want to purchase additional vials of the same donor's sperm once you conceive, so your children have the same donor/father. But you'll want to ask the bank whether there are storage fees involved and what your rights are if there's some sperm left over. Is it yours to give to a friend or sell? Can you donate it? What are the limitations? I've heard a few horror stories about clinics that were all too happy to take a client's money for a year's worth of sperm, only to severely restrict what the client could do with the leftovers.

Of course, you'll want to check out all their fees up front, too. If all you need is to have the vials delivered to your door, the fees will be in the hundreds of dollars per month. If you need more extensive services (intrauterine inseminations [IUI], which have a slightly better success rate than the old turkey-baster method, require that the sperm be washed, for example, and that you come into the clinic for inseminations), of course the fees will climb. With "older" parents (which usually means the woman is over thirty-five), it's pretty common to use sperm donation in conjunction with IVF. Of course, that will increase your costs substantially. Sometimes your insurance will cover the clinical procedures but not the sperm itself.

A less tangible factor, too, is just the general vibe you get from talking with the staff on the phone. You want to choose a place where you feel comfortable and respected.

If you're thinking of working with a sperm bank, try to get a referral from your doctor. If you happen to know other women and couples who have gone this route, ask them about their experiences.

I can't leave this topic without mentioning, too, that many, many women, notably some pioneering lesbians in the 1970s and 1980s, have been known to find a friend (or friend of a friend) to donate sperm, collect it in a sterilized jar, keep it warm, bring it home, and insert it into their own vaginas with a very clean turkey baster. Hey, if it works, and you're smart, careful, and thoughtful about how you do it, who am I to judge? But before you try this at home, please consider the potential emotional and legal complications that may result.

Here's the story of one couple who used a sperm donor.

Don and Sherry: Getting to Have a Baby Makes Everything Else Null and Void

My wife Sherry and I had been married for a year and trying to get pregnant from day one when we decided to get tested. She, luckily, was fine, but my tests showed low sperm count and motility issues.

My doctor said we could probably try IVF or IUI, but when we went back for the second test, the results were worse, and we were told they didn't think my sperm were suitable for either.

Our doctors recommended donor insemination for a variety of reasons. We could do it without putting my wife on all sorts of medications (as in IVF) or having her go through such an invasive procedure. From our research, we knew that the results were at least as good with a four- to six-month IUI program as with doing an IVF cycle. And, of course, there was the cost: We could afford to try IUI for a while and then still do an IVF if we wanted. But if we did an IVF, and it wasn't successful, we wouldn't be able to afford to do anything else.

We were very fortunate in that it took us only two tries, and my wife became pregnant with a baby girl.

For the most part, I look at it this way: My wife and I are having a baby, just with a little help. I feel like the father, and I'm sure that will continue after she is born. Most of our friends and family know what we are going through, which helps, too, because I can talk about it openly. There's a small part of me that was at first disappointed that we had to use a sperm donor, but that is totally separate from the joy of seeing my wife carrying our child and the anticipation of our beautiful baby girl being born.

I know everyone is different, but for my wife and me, we knew this was the right way to go and haven't regretted a moment of it. I know I am going to be a father, and my daughter will know how much I love her.

We plan on letting her know as much as she can understand as soon as possible, so she grows up with this information and considers it a normal part of her life. I am a little nervous about the inevitable questions about her donor (I hesitate to use dad *or* father, *even with "biological" in front of it). We have kept all the information about her donor and will support her curiosity in any way we can.*

I will be forever grateful to the man who donated his sperm and to the doctors and technology that allowed that to happen for us.

Sure, we have acquaintances who comment about the "unnaturalness" of inseminating my wife with another man's sperm. But it was the only way we were going to become parents, which made everything else null and void.

Donor Eggs

The situation with donor eggs is a little different. For starters, there's much more involved for the donor. With sperm donation, the donor doesn't have to take any special medications or undergo any complex harvesting procedures. Basically, all he has to do is come in and do the man thing into a sterilized cup. Egg donation, on the other hand, involves medications similar to those used for a regular IVF cycle to increase the number of eggs and embryos created and to time ovulation. For this and other reasons, it costs a lot more, too.

Sometimes, you can have the embryo that's created using the donor egg implanted into your own uterus and carry the baby yourself. Sometimes, you will need the donor (or another surrogate) to carry the baby for you. Additional issues to consider, and additional expenses.

Not only did Karen have the amazing good fortune of having a twin sister to donate eggs but her sister also ended up donating an ovary. I guess her story is only partially about egg donation, but it's such a good one that I had to include it.

Karen and Jami: The Unexpected Benefit of Being a Twin

In September 2005, I was diagnosed with premature ovarian failure (early menopause). I had all the symptoms, including hot flashes, dry skin, night sweats. I was not exactly a fun person to be around (my poor husband!); I was only twenty-five years old, and I had no chance at having children on my own.

Fortunately for me, I am an identical twin. When I found out that I was in menopause, I called up my twin sister, Jami, and explained that I needed some eggs. She didn't even hesitate. We decided to go through IVF using her eggs and my husband's sperm and then transferring the embryo to me. Since we are identical twins, we have the exact same DNA, which means that my eggs would have exactly the same genetic material as hers. We were told this situation was ideal.

Well, the IVF failed. It was the most horrible feeling in the world. My sister left work the day we found out and spent the whole day with me. She was as sad as I was.

Our next journey took us to St. Louis, where our doctor had referred us to a specialist who had performed ovarian transplants. In July 2006, my sister donated an entire ovary to me. The surgery is available only to identical twins because our bodies don't reject something with our own DNA. We were the sixth set of twins to ever have the surgery. Every time it has successfully worked to take a woman out of menopause.

I was unbelievably excited to get that first period after the surgery. I told everybody! Two weeks ago I found out that my follicle-stimulating hormone (FSH) level was down to 9 (it had been over

100 when I was in menopause). This is the first month that I have a chance of becoming pregnant on my own, no drugs, no doctors.

The doctors think that within the next year they should be able to do this surgery with anybody, not just identical twins.

Mike and Connie have an unusual story, too. It's one of the longer stories in this book, but I think you'll find it riveting. Their fertility problems started when they were quite young. Their story had lots of twists and turns, they had several children, and then they had a big surprise . . .

Connie and Mike's Story: You Never Know

Two years after Mike and I got married, I went off the Pill. I was just twenty-four and very healthy, and I really thought I would get pregnant that first time. When I didn't, I just figured it would happen the second time. Then the third. For months I continued to have faith that that would be the one for sure. And every month, my excitement would grow, my period would come, and my hope would plummet. The roller coaster was unbearable.

After six months, I told my gynecologist that I was concerned I wasn't conceiving. He told me to be patient and wait another six months. So, after another six long, emotional, and frustrating months, we sought additional help. My husband went to a urologist for an exam, which included a sperm count. It came back showing a low count and poor motility. The urologist also diagnosed a varicocele (an enlargement of the veins within the scrotum, which is believed to contribute to infertility) and recommended surgery. Before the surgery, the urologist asked if my workup had shown normal results. In our naïveté, we told him yes. In truth, no real workup had ever been done on me. Everyone just assumed that because I was twenty-five there could be no problem.

We were relieved by my husband's diagnosis. We figured we'd found the problem, and we could fix it.

He had the surgery, which was really awkward for us because we had kept everything a secret from our families. No one even knew we were trying to have children. We didn't talk about it because we were so sure it would end soon. We also didn't want a lot of questions. While my husband was recovering, I was put on a drug called Clomid to regulate my cycle and optimize the ovulation. We met with a fertility doctor, Dr. D, who suggested that we try intra-uterine insemination (IUI).

Thirty-six hours before our first attempt, I was given the necessary hCG shot (to control the timing of my ovulation). Meanwhile my husband had to give a sample of sperm at the urologist's office. The improvement wasn't dramatic, but the specimen was prepared for insemination anyway and then transferred to my uterus through a catheter. Then, we had to wait. . . . But we were optimistic. We really thought we had optimized our situation. We didn't realize how much lower the lows could get.

We did IUIs for eight months, at which point Dr. D suggested moving on to in vitro fertilization (IVF). With IVF, we were told, my husband's low motility and sperm count would not be as much of an issue.

Every night my husband had to give me an injection of hormones to stimulate my ovaries, and I was monitored regularly for blood hormone levels and given a sonogram to measure any growing eggs. At some point, we realized that the eggs were not growing to the desired measurement, and my blood levels were not up to expectations. They increased the level of medication to force the eggs to grow. Things did not look great, but some eggs were maturing, so the IVF was scheduled.

Once again, thirty-six hours before the procedure I had my shot of hCG to fully mature the few eggs that had developed. We saw thirteen eggs on the sonogram, but the estrogen level in my blood did not support that fact.

I was still hopeful.

The IVF procedure had a few parts. My husband delivered his specimen, and then, under sedation in the operating room (OR), I had my eggs extracted. The egg and sperm were then combined in a Petri dish, in the hopes that the eggs would fertilize. It's hard now to remember how emotional we felt about the whole idea that our child was going to be conceived without us present. It seems silly now that that was a concern, but it really did feel awful at the time.

Two or three days later, we came back to the OR to have the fertilized embryos placed in my uterus via catheter. We were told the embryos "didn't look great." They were apparently "fragmenting." But we would try anyway, because "you never know."

So with this thread of hope, we waited ten days, only to find out that I wasn't pregnant again. At this point, we were really devastated. We had invested so much emotion in the outcome of this procedure. We really thought this had to work. If not, what could it possibly mean? That there was no hope? We couldn't accept that. Plus our health insurance allowed only three IVF cycles, and we had just failed our first attempt. We had only two to go. Even then we knew we were lucky to have coverage at all, as the procedure and medications were expensive.

For logistical reasons, we had to wait a number of months before trying again, and that was really difficult. But we had time to come *out of our hole and begin to get ourselves in an optimistic frame of mind. We began to look forward to the next cycle. It was the only thing we could do.*

At this point, we had a new doctor. He evaluated our case and was shocked that I had not had any of the standard tests before my husband's surgery and the subsequent IUIs and IVF. He did not like the way my previous cycle had gone and wanted to reevaluate from scratch. So, I was sent for hysterosalpingography (HSG), where they inject dye into your uterus and fallopian tubes under X-ray guidance. This was to make sure everything was anatomically correct and that there were no blockages. We also had my blood levels drawn on day three of my period to check my hormone levels. I was shocked to find that one of my fallopian tubes was narrowed, and, even worse, that my FSH level was too high. Dr. G was very unenthusiastic about this news. He painted us a grim picture of our future.

Although we were only twenty-seven at this point, I felt under an incredible amount of pressure, timewise, and we had still not shared anything of this ordeal with our family or friends. We would cry secretly, together and apart. Unfortunately, this was all before the Internet. Research was hard to do, and there was no such thing as a chat room. And I was not prepared to sit in a group with live people discussing my issues.

My new doctor wanted to perform a laparoscopy to evaluate my reproductive organs from the inside. We scheduled this to coincide with a gamete intrafallopian transfer (GIFT) procedure, where the embryos would be placed directly into the good fallopian tube during the laparoscopy. Again, we were on a relative high. Embryos right into the tube—how could it get any closer?! Unfortunately, the whole cycle proceeded along the same route as the first. After the negative pregnancy test, Dr. G told me I would not be able to get pregnant this way. My body was acting like a forty-year-old's. He explained that the quality of my eggs was questionable and urged us to consider donor eggs or adoption.

I remember listening to him though a fog. I couldn't even believe he was talking to me. For years, everyone had said to us, "You're so young, don't worry." Now my twenty-seven-year-old body was not giving me any advantages. I remember leaving the office, getting into my car, and beginning to sob. This couldn't possibly be happening to me.

When my husband's problem had first been diagnosed, I had been kind of happy to think it was a "male problem." I was not to blame, it wasn't my fault. Now it was my fault. I really couldn't accept it.

I called my husband to tell him what the doctor had said. Then—I don't know how—I drove to meet him, and we stood out on the sidewalk crying in each other's arms.

After evaluating our options, we decided to look into egg donation. We felt that this would be a better initial choice over adoption, at least for us. The child would at least have my husband's genetic material, and I would get to be pregnant, carry, nurture, and give birth to our child. We convinced ourselves that this would work, as we had convinced ourselves so many times before.

We met with the staff psychologist to go over the procedure. We had to fill out forms. We had to choose what features we were looking for in a potential donor. It was very surreal to be making those choices. We chose hair and eye color to match ours, and the blood type had to at least match one of us.

No one would ever have to know we had done this. We thought no one could possibly understand. So much of our suffering was done alone. We never knew how many other people were going through the same ordeal. I don't know why I didn't think to get help or support. At the time, it just seemed better to keep it to ourselves. Then, we waited.

In the meantime, we went on with life, and kept trying the natural way. The doctors had said it could still happen, "you never know." We decided we needed to get away and planned a three-week vacation out of the country. As we sat in the airport waiting to board our flight, we checked phone messages back in our apartment and were shocked to find a message from the medical center stating that they had a possible egg donor who matched our requirements. What should we do? Cancel our trip? Was that the right question to even be asking? Were we really ready to give up on having our own biological child?

We decided to call Dr. G. For the first time since we had met him, he actually gave us some hope. He suggested we use the donation and try "just one more time."

When we got back from vacation, we got down to business. We had only one more IVF available to us on our health insurance. Dr. G sent us to a lab that was using a new technology called ICSI, where they would inject the sperm directly into the egg to fertilize it, and they were having much success.

Ironically, they placed me on the Pill for two weeks prior to beginning the follicle stimulation. The cycle didn't fare much better than the previous two. The eggs were slow to grow, and my estrogen levels were borderline. The director of the program suggested canceling the cycle, but our doctor convinced him that I was very young and that that was how my body worked, and he let us stick it out. I

ICSI was developed in the early 1990s. Before that time, men with poor sperm needed to use a donor.

---

believe they retrieved only seven eggs. We waited for news of fertilization. We were told the embryos weren't doing too well. We had to wait until the morning of the scheduled transfer to see if the embryos were growing properly. Another lovely roller coaster ride. We sat by the phone waiting. Finally we got the call and were told to come in. They would transfer whatever they had, because "you never know."

When we got to the hospital we found out we had two "crappy" embryos. One was doing slightly better than the other, but they would both be transferred. I remember lying in recovery, with my pelvis elevated, afraid to move, for fear of having the embryos fall out before having a chance to attach to my uterine lining (which was doing very well, by the way. That's something they check on, too.).

Ten days later I went for my pregnancy blood test. My breasts didn't feel as tender as they had the day before. That was a bad sign. I was sure it meant a period was coming and broke down and sobbed hysterically on the shoulder of an office mate. (I had told her what was going on so that she could cover for me.) She comforted me and calmed me down. Then began the long wait for the phone call from the nurse with the results. I had convinced myself the call didn't matter because the news was just going to be like all the rest.

Calls were usually made at around three o'clock. I knew that they made the "good" calls first and the "bad" news calls after. When I hadn't received my call by 4:30, I felt that same desperation rise in my throat. I was at work but kept checking my home answering machine. Nothing.

Finally, I shut the door to my office and called them myself. "Hi, I haven't received the blood work results yet," I told the nurse.

"Just hold on," she replied.

The wait seemed interminable. She came back on the line and asked me if I was sitting down. That had to be bad. I replied yes. "You're pregnant," she said.

I was astounded. "What?" I asked. I couldn't believe my ears. I was virtually in shock. Four long years we had waited for this moment. "Don't tell anyone yet," the nurse said. "We have to make sure the hormone levels rise properly, and then we want to see a heartbeat." I didn't even care. I was pregnant! Was it really possible?

I called my husband immediately, and through my tears and sobs I told him the news.

"Are you crying because you are, or are you crying because you aren't?" he asked. "I can't understand you." He was in a crowd of his colleagues in a busy hallway. "I am, I am, I am!" I cried, trying to keep my voice low so that my entire office couldn't hear.

I went to meet him at a small ceremony where he was due to get an award. The entire ride there, I had a stupid smile on my face. Then I thought about the crappy little embryo that could. I pictured it clawing its way into my beautiful uterine lining and hanging on for dear life. I knew that if we had come so far, God was not going to take it away from us now!

The auditorium was crowded, and my husband was seated far away from me, but we locked eyes across the large room. We smiled at each other. We had a secret. As soon as he got his award, he made his way to me, and we hugged like crazy and cried. Everyone thought I was so proud of him and his silly little award. They had no idea.

Nine months later we gave birth to a beautiful baby girl.

Although it sounds crazy, we couldn't wait to try again. Dr. G suggested we try as soon as we were physically ready, because time was working against us. So, when our daughter was only seven months old, we began another IVF cycle. I remember feeling guilty, coming for my blood work and sonograms. I had to bring my daughter with me sometimes. I saw the other women sitting there. I wondered if they were thinking "Why is she here?" Or would they feel comforted knowing "It worked for her, it might work for me?" I never spoke to any of them. I felt uncomfortable that I wasn't one of them anymore.

For this next IVF cycle, though, we had the magic recipe. The right timing, the right doses of medication, the right laboratory. We also had the same crappy cycle and same crappy embryos, but nine months later we had our second child, a son. While we were on a roll, we decided to take our chances and try one more time. We felt that emotionally, we had nothing to lose. We were parents. We had two children, a boy and a girl. Our new health insurance allowed us two IVF cycles and we had used only one.

The cycle went much like all the others, except the quality of the eggs had much improved. We were actually discouraged from transferring all four embryos, because my history was so positive. Wasn't that the irony of all ironies? Again, I got pregnant and had another son. We were so ecstatic. Our friends unknowingly began to call me Fertile Myrtle. If only they knew!

During the third cycle, I made friends with a woman who was undergoing IVF for the second time. Her first time ended in a miscarriage. We shared war stories. It made me realize how alone my husband and I had been through the whole process. It was great to talk to someone who knew what I was going through. She actually told me I was her inspiration. It made me feel great, and a little sad about how alone I had been. Although, in retrospect, I don't know if I could have done it any other way.

When my youngest turned two, I was thirty-five years old. I began to wonder if I wanted one more child, but I didn't think I could go through another IVF procedure emotionally. We decided to let nature and fate take its course. I had not used birth control in ten

*years, so I really didn't think it would happen. But, as the doctors
had always told us, "You never know."*

My husband and I decided to go away for a weekend. Much as
we adored our family, it was great to get away, alone. We had a
great time. Twenty-nine days later, I still had not gotten my period.
Not that it was "late," but out of habit I called my husband and
asked him to pick up a pregnancy test. We both knew that the surest
way to bring on my period was to take a pregnancy test. But, never
one to deny me, he stopped at the drugstore and picked one up.
While we had been "trying," I would let him buy only a name-
brand expensive test. This time I told him not to spend the extra
money and just get the store brand.

He came home and handed me the test and I went and used it
immediately. I watched for the little line to show that the test was
working. Then I had to wait three or five minutes, so I put the test
down on the floor. When I came back to it a couple of minutes later,
wouldn't you know the second blue line had appeared! I had waited
seven years for that blue line, and there it was. It was just as thrilling
as the phone call from the nurse. In fact, it was kind of strange not to
have a third party involved!

I opened the bathroom door with a silly grin on my face. I found
my husband in a bedroom with the kids. He looked at me expectantly, and I nodded and started to cry. My daughter wanted to
know why I was crying, and my husband told her it was because
"Mommy loves all of you so much."

Our daughter is nearly ten years old. Our sons are eight, six, and
four. Our families still don't know the truth. We often wonder how
we will ever tell them, or if we even should. I think we will tell our
children at some point down the road. It will be their news to share.
For now though, whenever we hear that a couple is struggling to

have children, we take them aside, show them the pictures in our wallet, and tell them about our little secrets.

Connie and Mike were very lucky. They were matched with an egg donor by their doctor, and got pregnant the first time out. She doesn't even mention the donor, and obviously the choice of donor was not particularly fraught. But there can be lots of twists and turns with donation of either kind. With egg donation you'll want to consider beforehand how many embryos you want to implant each cycle and what you will do with any "leftovers," because, as with IVF, you will not be making just one embryo per cycle. Probably more like five, six, or eight.

This is just like with IVF, but this time you are involving at least one other person. And that means that the questions, choices, and decisions you will need to make along the way have the potential to be that much more complicated—by your personal morals, ethics, and belief system and sometimes by hers. So once again, communication is imperative.

> There are important legal ramifications to any donor/surrogate relationship. So get good legal advice from someone with expertise in these areas.

What, for instance, do you think about donating unused embryos? Maybe you'd be fine with it, or would you forever be afraid of being contacted later in life by a resulting child? The ideal solution for you may not be the same for your partner or for the egg/sperm donor or surrogate assisting you.

There are also legal ramifications to any donor/surrogate relationship. *So get good legal advice from someone with expertise in these areas.*

As much as I (or anyone else for that matter) can tell you, there is *no substitute for doing your own research*. You can't make the choices right for *you* based on someone else's advice or information.

Single Mothers by Choice— and Other Heroes

When I hear stories of what some women and men go through to create their families, I realize how lucky Guy and I were. We never had to venture past our own biological material, and we always had each other. My own doctor began preparing to build a family as a single parent using a sperm donor (then ended up marrying and conceiving through IVF). The National Organization of Single Mothers (NOSM), an organization founded by syndicated columnist Andrea Engber, estimates that there are more than *13 million* single mothers today raising America's children. Of course many of these women had their children within a marriage and then became single, but Engber claims that the fastest growing group is what she calls "mothers outside of marriage," a group "whose rate for educated women in their late twenties and mid-thirties has tripled in the past decade." These are women who don't at all fit the stereotype of the woman who "couldn't find a man."

With the divorce rate up, the marriage rate down, and increasing numbers of single women wanting to start families whether or not they've found Mr. Right, it's easy to see how this could happen. We no longer wait for the perfect circumstances, particularly as our biological clocks keep ticking.

I cannot tell you how in awe I am of women who choose to take charge of their own lives in this way. To plan and to meet your personal family-building goals all on your own—well, it just takes my breath away. These women are seriously my heroes. They inspire me daily as I struggle to be a good mother with all the help and resources that having a great partner and supportive family provide.

As banks and clinics open all over the country at an amazing rate, I feel grateful. It's all good news to those of us who are unable to realize our baby dreams the old-fashioned way.

For Guy and me, the journey through infertility was difficult enough without the added stresses of trying to conceive either as a single parent or as a gay, lesbian, or nontraditional family. Even in the best of cases, infertility is a crazy ride in which you have to fight each day to maintain your personal sense of value, stability, and self-esteem. Going it alone, it seems to me, is like choosing the biggest, highest, and fastest roller coaster in the park. You'd better be prepared for a wild ride.

Resources

FERTILITY PLUS
www.fertilityplus.com

This is a grassroots, patient-to-patient site for people trying to conceive. Its purpose is not to dispense medical advice but to pass along information and personal experiences on donor sperm, donor egg, surrogacy, and "embryo adoption" issues and resources.

SPERMBANKDIRECTORY.COM
www.spermbankdirectory.com

This site has a ton of information about sperm banks and links to banks all over the country.

EGG DONATION, INC.
15821 Ventura Boulevard
Suite 675
Encino, CA 91436
818-385-0950
www.eggdonor.com

This organization's website can direct you to an egg donor and provides information about the process and the legal and financial issues involved.

INTERNET HEALTH RESOURCES
www.ihr.com

The site contains information and resources for egg and sperm donation.

CHOICE MOMS
www.choosingsinglemotherhood.com

This is the website of author Mikki Morrissette. It was originally developed to promote her book *Choosing Single Motherhood* but has since become a great resource for single mothers by choice, which is one of the fastest-growing populations seeking medical assistance with pregnancy.

NATIONAL ASSOCIATION OF SINGLE MOTHERS (NOSM)
www.singlemothers.org

This is the official site of NOSM, a group formed to help "single moms by choice or chance face the daily challenges of life with wisdom, wit, dignity, confidence and courage." It is also home of the award-winning quarterly *Single Mother: A Support Group in Your Hands.*

ERICKSON LAW
Theresa Erickson, Esq.
12780 Danielson Court
Suite B
Poway, CA 92064
866-757-4994
www.ericksonlaw.net

Mission statement: "We are a professional firm committed to providing high quality, personalized surrogacy, egg donation, embryo donation, sperm donation advice, representation and related legal services to help couples and individuals create the family that they have always wanted. We provide open, semi-anonymous and anonymous arrangements. Each client's confidentiality is absolutely assured."

CHAPTER 8

Beyond Biology: Creating Your Family Through Adoption

Of course, there is one more route to creating a family, and that's adoption. Well over 100,000 children are adopted in the United States each year. There are a great many resources available on adoption, including lots and lots of books, websites, and organizations, so I won't go into any of the technical or legal issues. But I do want to say a few things about making this profound choice.

First of all, as you probably know, there are several different types of adoption—open (when at least the birth mother is known and sometimes the father), closed (when she is not), domestic, international, and fost-adopt. Each comes with its own set of very personal considerations.

Some people are lucky enough to be present at the birth of their babies, others adopt infants or toddlers, others open their lives to older children who desperately need the stability of family. I've even known some couples who adopted the babies of relatives who couldn't care for them. Because many babies up for adoption are non-white and many couples looking to adopt are white, there are many transracial families formed by adoption. And these come with their own set of complicated social and political concerns. Some people very deliberately choose to adopt kids with special needs. And, finally, some people adopt even when they don't "have to" (see Bob's story later in this chapter) and many do so after long and difficult efforts at getting pregnant. No matter what brings people to the decision to adopt, as I see it, all of them are heroes.

I won't even try to touch on the procedures involved in adoption. I'm just not an expert on this, and as I said earlier, there are so many resources available to you if you choose this route. I can say go with your gut and don't feel pressured to follow anyone else's path. Do what's right for you and your family. *But do your homework!* As in every other arena, there are good agencies and bad; there are things you need to know to get your own house in order; and there are financial considerations involved in each kind of adoption (from the relatively free public domestic adoption to the five-figure international). Unlike the process of bearing your own child, the process of adopting is a little more invasive. The state gets involved, and you have to put up with the indignity of being evaluated to see whether you are fit to parent, with having your home visited, and with undergoing social worker visits.

Guy and I discussed adoption for a only a brief period between Nicholas's birth and our one failed in vitro fertilization (IVF) attempt before we had the girls. He was not totally onboard with the idea, not ready to give up the fight to have our own biological children. Had it been our only option we might well have chosen this path from the start. I might have spent more time and more effort to research the outlets that would have been available to us. As it was, however, surrogacy intervened—and the rest, as they say, is history. Our family is now complete; however, I have to say, should the urge to raise another child come up again in the future, I'm not so sure we wouldn't revisit adoption.

Whether or not they are linked to us biologically, children remind us that there are no boundaries around our ability to love and that life is full of unexpected opportunities. There are certainly many children the world over who urgently need loving, stable homes and parents who will offer them the love and constancy and attention they deserve.

The experience of adoption can be as emotionally intense as anything you will experience in life. I've watched friends and family struggle with the very highs and the very lows of this type of journey as well. The stories included here illustrate that far better than any further words that I can offer.

Bob: Can I Love a Child Not My Own?

The turbulent '70s, with Vietnam, racial strife, and women's lib, was not the best of times to start a nontraditional family. My wife, Doris, and I already had one child and there was no medical reason why we couldn't have more. It was Doris who initially came up with the idea to adopt a child. When she told me, I was not comfortable at all.

What would our parents think, and what would the neighbors say? Would they think that there was something medically wrong with me? To compound matters, she suggested we look into Korean international adoptions because we could get a healthy infant in around nine months (as compared to a private domestic adoption, which could take years). Now add to my fears a child who would look radically different from me and dealing with other people's prejudices. But the most fearful anxiety of all was that I was not sure I could love another child as my own.

I confided my trepidations to a good friend of mine, and he told me of a relation of his who had recently adopted a Korean baby girl. After making contact, we were invited to talk with them about the adoption process and to meet their daughter, Ginny. I remember sweating profusely and being sick to my stomach on the way over to their house. We knocked on the door, and when it opened there stood two-year-old Ginny clutching a teddy bear in one hand and her mother's leg with the other. Her black eyes stared at us, not sure if we were friend or foe. At that moment, my fear melted away and adoption suddenly seemed like a very real possibility.

Paperwork, money, and interviews consumed our lives for the next several months. We worked with an international adoption agency and a local agency and did whatever it took to see our way through the process. All our personal references were checked—even our five-year-old daughter was not immune to being interviewed and questioned—and a complete dossier was compiled. Our file was then submitted to the international agency, and we awaited approval.

It came in the form of a letter. We were approved! And advised that because there was a higher demand for infant girls, we could have a long wait. So we opted for a boy. The search was on. It seemed like forever before we got a call telling us they had found a child and his information was being mailed to us.

Two pictures and a one-page letter arrived a short while later. This was all the history there was for eight-month-old Chul Qu Park. His mother had died in childbirth, and his father was unknown. His grandmother was too old to care for him and had brought him to the orphanage.

I carried around his picture, with his wonderful inquisitive smile, like a mother carrying her child to birth, and felt connected to this child long before his actual arrival. (I still carry around that picture to this day.) For me, this added dimension was the best part of the adoption process.

But it was also the worst. Suppose he got sick? What if the paperwork got lost? What if the powers-that-be changed their minds and decided to send another child? The bonding process had already started and along with it came the rational and irrational worrying.

But the day finally came when he was to arrive. I waited with my daughter back home while Doris flew to Chicago to pick him up. A charter flight with about thirty Korean children landed to emotional pandemonium. My wife flew back that same night to bring our new baby home. Seeing them walk through the airport was the culmination of many months of an amazingly emotional trip. I have not experienced anything like it since. Holding this tired, frightened little boy for the first time proved that yes, I could love another child as my own.

In so many respects, Bob's journey, while obviously profound, was rather simple. He and his wife did not endure the stresses and financial drain of infertility and had the privilege of *choosing*, very freely, to adopt. Bob obviously had emotional issues to work through, and I find his story of finding his son very inspiring. Perhaps Bob's story will inspire some of you to spare yourselves the difficulties of lengthy and expensive infertility treatments and choose the adoption route from the get-go. There are so many children out there who need the love we have to offer. But I'm guessing most of the readers of this book will better relate to the experience of my friend Erika, who took an entirely different and more grueling road to adoption.

Erika: If Only I'd Thought of It Sooner!

Erika and her husband tried and tried to have a baby on their own. At first they had a blast having reckless unprotected sex after years of being on the Pill. But after many months without success and a rapidly dwindling sense of fun—and with terribly painful and heavy periods, to boot—Erika went to see her doctor, who put her on Clomid. Unfortunately, he did not have her chart her cycles or do any tests to see if she was ovulating. Month after difficult month on Clomid, to which she had a not-atypical reaction of feeling like a raving lunatic, she expected to get pregnant with the help of the drug. The doses were increased a few times. Still no luck. Now she can laugh at herself, but at the time she thought that shelling out $75 a month for the Clomid was hard. Little did she know what awaited her.

She started making deals with God. She prayed to God every night to let her get pregnant, always wondering what she had "done wrong in life to be punished like this." She reached out to old friends to make amends—anything to realize her dream.

It wasn't until she found herself envying a soldier on TV who was broadcasting a greeting to his wife and children back home from his barracks in Iraq that she realized she was hitting bottom. She had developed tunnel vision.

Several visits to a new doctor later and still on large doses of Clomid, she discovered that she had a "hostile uterus." In other words, there was something chemical going on in her uterus that killed her husband's otherwise-healthy sperm. Not the words a woman on hormones for a year wants to hear!

She then had an hysterosalpingogram (HSG), which showed nothing abnormal, and proceeded to try a few rounds of intra-uterine inseminations (IUIs). Still no pregnancy.

After endometriosis was diagnosed (discovered through some routine testing before trying in vitro), she underwent a surgical procedure to remove the wayward endometrial tissue, and the surgery left her in a great deal of pain from internal bleeding.

After several IVFs and a terribly difficult miscarriage, Erika and her husband began to seriously reconsider their options. I'll let Erika take over from here.

During this time of sorrow I had to take a step back and really evaluate my life. Could we endure any more of this pain? Why was I putting my body and my spirit through this? How much more could my husband and I take both emotionally and financially? And when it came right down to it, the only answer I could come up with was that I had never failed at anything I had set out to do in my life. And darn it, I wasn't going to fail at pregnancy either.

But after finally achieving a pregnancy and still seeing the bottom fall out, well, that was when I realized that what we wanted most of all was to become parents. Did it really matter if the child was linked to us genetically? It didn't to me. It was time to have a heart-to-heart, and it turned out it didn't matter one lick to my wonderful husband either.

It was then and there that we decided to adopt. It seemed so obvious. My aunt had adopted all four of her children; I had two other cousins who had adopted as well. And they all had wonderful families! Why, oh why, hadn't we ever discussed adoption?

We took about a year off from trying to have a baby, and we saved our money, and we worked on ourselves. I had come to detest my body in ways I never want to feel again. It had let me down time and time again, and I needed to get back in tune with liking it. I started exercising religiously. I joined a yoga class and went three times a week and ran on the treadmill the other days. I got into pretty good shape, and I made peace with my body. I got back in a good place spiritually too during this time. The years of infertility treatment had wreaked havoc not only on my body but on my spirituality. I mentioned earlier the deals I tried to make with God. Well, after the miscarriage, I actually lost faith for a while. I really and truly couldn't believe that any loving God could let one couple endure so much pain. I needed this time to heal before embarking on the journey that would eventually lead us to the daughter that was meant to be ours all along.

We went on that next year to research adoption. We looked into the different kinds of adoptions: domestic, international, open, closed—you name it. We read books and called agencies. In the spring we went to an adoption seminar that one of the agencies was putting on. It was the first one we went to, and we expected to go to many more before we found the right agency. But that first night we knew they were a good match for us, and we immediately got the paperwork started.

We chose to pursue an open adoption. We worked on our paperwork and made our picture profile (which potential birth parents would look at) over the summer. It was a busy time but also an exciting time. We had to write our individual biographies, and we had to fill out form after form for the agency. We also had to ask four of our closest friends and family members to write letters of recommendation for us. I couldn't believe how eager they were to do this for us, and I cried reading each one of them. It was amazing how much our friends and family wanted us to become parents as well.

When that was all complete, we made an appointment for a social worker to come into our home to do our home study. It ended up being very painless and easy—more like a visit with an old friend. But you couldn't have told me ahead of time that it would end up being like that. I had our home scrubbed from top to bottom. I spent one entire weekend putting our heating vents through the dishwasher for fear that there was dust on them! I even went out and bought a coffee pot just in case the social worker might want a cup of coffee during her visit.

I was so terrified that she would come into our home and deem us unfit somehow to adopt a baby. But she came, looked around a bit, and then sat down across from us on the couch and talked and talked and talked. She asked us about our upbringings, about our hopes and dreams, about what we see our future family life to be like, etc. It was painless, and by the time she left we felt like old friends. She came to our home three times before she wrote up her report that would be turned into our agency okaying us as future adoptive parents.

One beautiful, cold, crisp day in November, four years into the process, we returned home from a day out with friends to find a message on our answering machine. It was from our agency saying that a potential birth mother and birth father had just come into the agency and they thought we might be a perfect fit. Our caseworker gave us all the information about these potential birth parents and then told us to hang up the phone, talk about whether or not we thought it was a good match for us, and then call her back. We only had to look at each other to know. We told her instantly that we didn't need to talk about it. Everything she had told us had sounded perfect. We just felt in our hearts and souls that this match was right. She was thrilled and said she would arrange a meeting.

We met the following weekend at a restaurant. I was a nervous wreck and I do believe my husband had a case of the nerves too. So many things go through your mind. . . . Will they like us? What if they meet us and then change their minds? What will we say to each other? How will I keep myself from crying? On our way there our caseworker prepped us on what things to say and not to say. She told us not to make statements as if the baby were already ours. She cautioned us to follow their lead in the conversation and talk about them (their likes, hobbies, etc.) and to steer clear of any probing questions, keeping the conversation light. She also suggested that we have some baby names ready in case they wanted to know them, but not to bring that up unless they asked. It would be polite and considerate, she said, to ask if they had any name preferences that they wanted us to consider. We felt better after we got there and as it turned out the match was even better than I could have imagined.

These were the kind of people who would have been our friends had we met them at a different place and time and under different *circumstances. We laughed and had a great conversation the entire time. Never did the meal feel awkward or forced. I was actually sad when the dinner was over, and we had to leave them. We hugged good-bye and thanked them for meeting with us. The next time we would see each other was at the hospital for the baby's birth. We would have loved to have spent more time with them, but we also knew how hard that would have been on them.*

Things went along well, and we arranged to be at the hospital for the birth of our daughter. We got there early and waited in the hospital waiting room with our caseworker for what seemed like days but was actually just a few hours. Minutes after the birth, our daughter's birth father came into the waiting room and said these exact words: "Congratulations, you have a daughter." I have never felt such joy in my life! He asked us if we were ready to come and meet her and I immediately started crying. I was overwhelmed with emotions. We were finally going to meet this little person, the baby we had been hoping and praying for for so long.

She was absolutely beautiful, and it was as if the years of pain melted away instantly. Here she was. The one. We had been waiting for her all this time.

We were holding her within fifteen minutes of her birth, and we got to experience her first bath and her first bottle as well. Later that day, Abigail's birth father came back down to see us. He told us that he had always heard people talking about someone's face "lighting up" but that he had never actually seen that happen until he walked into the waiting room and told me that our baby had been born.

Those years of infertility rocked me to my core. Loving Abigail and becoming her mother and watching her personality grow with each day has made me realize that I do believe, without a doubt, that

Abigail was meant to be with my husband and me. And I know that her birth parents feel the same way. They have made us feel in no uncertain terms that "things happen for a reason," and they are happy that they could be a part of this. Faith renewed. Spirit restored.

The journey to parenthood was hard, to say the least, but it was worth every single minute. I wouldn't change a thing about what happened in the past. It was our journey. Our marriage is stronger, and I was still able to see my husband become that wonderful father I always knew he would be. Our daughter is the light of our lives, and we couldn't love her more. I feel fortunate that those feelings of pain melted away when Abigail was placed in our arms. Adoption was right for us.

Private or public, domestic or international, transracial, trans-cultural, open or closed, there are now so many ways to adopt that can make your baby dreams come true. Please don't rule out this very important option.

Resources

NATIONAL ADOPTION CENTER
1500 Walnut Street
Suite 701
Philadelphia, PA 19102
800-TO-ADOPT
www.adopt.org

Mission statement: "The National Adoption Center expands adoption opportunities for children living in foster care throughout the United States, and is a resource to families and to agencies who seek the permanency of caring homes for children."

AMERICAN ADOPTIONS
9101 West 110th Street
Second floor, Suite 200
Overland Park, KS 66210
800-ADOPTION
www.americanadoptions.com

Mission statement: "American Adoptions is currently one of the largest non-profit licensed domestic adoption agencies in the United States completing over 300 adoptions annually. As a non-profit, licensed adoption agency American Adoption provides a full range of services to adoptive families and birth parents across the country."

CHILDREN'S HOPE INTERNATIONAL
11780 Borman Drive
St. Louis, MO 63146
314-890-0086
www.childrenshopeint.org

Mission statement: "We are a full service licensed, not for profit 501(C)(3) adoption and humanitarian agency, accredited by the COA and Hague pursuant. Well organized in each country where we assist families in adopting, our work is based on relationships that have been established for many years throughout the world. We are accredited by the Council on Accreditation which is the highest level possible for a placement agency. Children's Hope was one of the first agencies to receive Accreditation by the Russian Ministry of Education to legally place children from that country."

HUMAN RIGHTS CAMPAIGN
www.hrc.org

This site devotes a section to adoption agencies that are open to lesbian and gay individuals and couples.

THE NORTH AMERICAN COUNCIL ON ADOPTABLE CHILDREN
970 Raymond Avenue
Suite 106
St. Paul, MN 55114
651-644-3036
www.nacac.org

"Founded in 1974 by adoptive parents, the North American Council on Adoptable Children is committed to meeting the needs of waiting children and the families who adopt them.... Thousands of children cannot remain with their birth families. These children—once labeled unadoptable or hard to place—are mostly school-aged. Some are brothers and sisters who must be placed together. Others are drug-exposed or medically fragile. Most have physical, mental or emotional difficulties. Many are children of color. All need loving families."

COMMONWEALTH ADOPTIONS INTERNATIONAL
877-311-4646
www.commonwealthadoption.org

"Commonwealth Adoptions International specializes in international adoption to help orphaned children overseas find safe, loving homes. Recently, Commonwealth Adoptions has started a domestic adoption program to assist children in the US find forever families as well."

PART 3

Where Do You Go from Here?

CHAPTER 9

A Guy's Perspective

I thought it might be illuminating to include some insights on the infertility experience from a guy—that is, from my husband, Guy.

Guy Speaks: Is Anyone Out There Listening?

Something as basic as not getting your wife pregnant is definitely a blow to the male ego. No argument. And for sure there are big differences between men and women in general and how we handle this news. We're all wired differently. Even within the male species you've got all different kinds of guys. You've got the guys who are jealous and crazy, the kind who say wild things like, "My son will come from me come hell or high water." And then there are your normal, rational men, the guys I met during the whole in vitro thing, who just want the kids. When you get down to it, it is that simple, isn't it? We want kids. However we get them. The ends justify the means. . . .

When this bomb first hit us, it was like, okay, we've got a problem, let's solve it. I don't get gray or emotional about situations like this. It was like—here are the facts, let's deal with them. I mean it was awful. Don't get me wrong. When the doctor came in the very first time and told us our first results were negative, and I was there with Cindy in the room as she heard those words and started to cry, believe me—it was freakin' awful! But I knew we would try again. I knew we would find a way to afford it, and I knew that Cindy was committed to it. (We in fact ended up financing the last two in vitro fertilizations [IVFs] and taking out a second mortgage for the surrogacy). So as hard as it was that we had failed the first time, I still knew that we'd get there.

The hardest part is the initial shock that you failed. Because you go in and think you've done everything right. You've followed all the instructions to the letter. You're not prepared for the failure of it. But after the second failure, I literally started looking at it like calculus. Okay, that took four months and sixteen grand. We'll take a month off and do it again. We'll need this many shots, this many doctor appointments. It just became like a job. Like building one of my restaurants. This is what it takes to get my kid. Okay.

We actually blew it four times. That's hard. But I always knew that when Cindy was ready we'd do it again. And the truth is, it actually got easier for me each time, as strange as that sounds. The first time was the hardest for sure.

I was very supportive of Cindy throughout the whole thing, never fearful of any of the in vitro testing or procedures. But I can't say I know what it was like for her. You'll hear women talk about the forty hours of labor, the difficult birth, the shots, the pain, all of that—and they never really forget the experience. You never hear men talking about that stuff because, frankly, men just don't re-

member. Women have much more of a connection to having a baby because of what they do. The physical part. Even the whole first year after your baby is born, it's still mostly the mother who carries the burden. By the time our kids get to age one or two and we fathers start kicking in, we're so far beyond the point of caring where they came from or how they got here. At that point, we're just fathers who want to play basketball with our sons or be the apple in our little girl's eye.

After Nicholas, we knew we wanted more children, but we also knew that we needed a fertile woman to carry them. We had no trouble producing the eggs and sperm, but for whatever reason, Cindy's uterus kept rejecting our embryos. I guess I could have freaked out, but I just went into reality mode. Frankly, I was afraid for Cindy's health. Her body had undergone so many chemically in-duced changes, not to mention the whole mind game that you have to play with yourself and with each other as you try to get through each attempt. So we made the decision to make one last bunch of good embryos and put them into Shannon, our surrogate. Problem solved.

At one point we considered adoption, and I'm not going to lie to you, the idea weirded me out a little. Cindy was much more into trying to adopt than I was. With IVF and surrogacy we were always still talking about our kids. Cindy's eggs, my sperm. No conflict. Don't get me wrong. Adoption is such an amazing thing—that any-body would do that is so incredible, but I couldn't get past the fact that the kid wouldn't really be mine. Part of me felt bad, but we have friends who have adopted, and you're happy and you love your kids and all, but it's more of a struggle, the first few years especially.

Most of the people I know who say they could never do a surro-gate already have kids of their own. But when you've been put in a

situation in which someone tells you, guess what, you can't get preg-
nant, you just think differently. Most people think of in vitro like it's
a visit to the witch doctor. But you know what, if you had to go
through it, if you had no other choice, you'd look at it another way.
That's just the way it is.

Whether my child was in Cindy's womb or Shannon's didn't
matter to me. They were still my girls, and I wasn't going to be read-
ing them bedtime stories or kissing them good night until they got
here.

Sure, it was a little strange to have another woman involved, but
the hard part for me was the financial pressure. Surrogacy is ex-
tremely costly. Lots more than an in vitro procedure, and more so for
us because our surrogate was in Minnesota, and the back-and-forth
travel alone was expensive. A lot of financial pressure on me. But as
for the decision to go the surrogacy route—well, I look at the girls
now and, quite honestly, I forget about the part Shannon played.

The girls are our biological children and maybe that plays a role,
too. I don't know. I just know that for me—for a man—once the
kid is here, how it got here is over. Really, you never think of those
things again.

Guy and I went through much of our infertility journey as
many couples do, focusing most of our attention on me and what
I was going through. After all, women are on the receiving end of
most of the poking and prodding, emotionally and physically, and
men often get lost in the shuffle. There were many times in our
journey when Guy felt that sense of not belonging. What he says
is absolutely true; he is a man very steeped in reality. He is one of
those people who oozes a sense of calm; his actions are determined
and precise. But that doesn't spare him hurt. Yes, it allowed him to

channel his energy into action, in a more immediate and positive way. I think that's definitely a guy thing.

Women, I think, actually crave the *feeling* of being pregnant and feel the loss more acutely when we can't conceive. It's *our* bodies, after all. Men can't really relate to that part. I mean, I believe they feel it, but for many reasons they react differently and usually less outwardly. They might feel the same sense of loss, but they don't have the same outlets for expressing their confusion, embarrassment, or fears. This can leave them feeling kind of resentful of the reality that has taken over life as they once knew it.

Our friend Glen and his wife found out about his male factor infertility years into their process of trying to conceive. And he's haunted by the guilt. Of course, a good doctor or specialist might have suggested that he be tested(!), but alas that didn't happen. He describes his own reaction so poignantly.

Glen and Debbie: If I'd Only Known . . .

Most men with fertility problems have no signs or symptoms. Sure, there are the few that experience outward signs that tip them off early on: hormonal problems that cause a change in their voice or pattern of hair growth, enlargement of their breasts, or difficulty with sexual function. But most of us have no clues. Unfortunately, I was the problem for over five years before I even thought to be tested, assuming—like most men do—that the problem must surely lie within the confines of those mystery places in my wife. Had I been more attentive, had a doctor (or my wife) even hinted, we could have saved ourselves years of tortuous procedures and emotionally draining experiences.

The guilt of that time is overwhelming. If I had known, would I have stepped up readily? Accepted the blame? Endured the heartache as readily? Frankly, I don't think so.

My wife says she forgives me. But when I look at our daughter (born through donor sperm), I pray that she will one day have a more sensitive and giving partner.

The stress infertility can place on a marriage is unbelievable, as I mentioned early in the book. My friend James and his wife, Mary, didn't make it. James was so committed to the process, but, as James said to me once, infertility is as much about survival as it is about success.

James and Mary had two beautiful children, but they lost each other in the process. Whenever I read James's description of his infertility journey, I am struck by how precisely and honestly he captures the process.

James and Mary's Story: When "Natural" Doesn't Happen

My marriage to Mary did not survive our infertility ordeal. We tried for over five years before having our children and went through some incredible trials. I will always be grateful, because I have two beautiful daughters, but I miss out on so much of their lives. I'm not sure what I would have done differently if I could do it all over, but I surely would have gone to greater lengths to keep my marriage intact.

Here's what I remember: At some point Mary went to see her OB/GYN because we weren't having any luck on our own. I could kick myself now, but she went alone. We didn't even talk about having me come along, too. After examining her and asking lots of questions, the doctor suggested she do hysterosalpingography (HSG) to check her fallopian tubes for blockages. They found "nothing wrong." She started taking ovulation drugs and prenatal vitamins, and we started doing artificial inseminations.

I'll never forget the first time the nurse handed me a cup and just pointed to a restroom door. It wasn't as easy as you'd think! We also tried collecting my sperm samples at home. The most hilarious part was trying not to spill any. I had never before (or since) thought of my sperm as so precious!

We tried artificial insemination a number of times, and it just wasn't working. Every month we'd get our hopes up so high, only to experience that crashing sense of failure when it didn't work. Finally, our OB/GYN referred us to a specialist, telling us there was "nothing more" he could do.

We plunged headlong into researching the right clinic. It seemed as if there were a million of them. How do you choose? We ended up visiting several for consultations, and then just trusted our guts on the one that "felt" the best.

Then there was the whole ordeal of having to give Mary the shots. For me, that was the most difficult part of all, preparing the shots daily, doing the injections, and seeing the pain I was inflicting. I really hated it.

The clinic we were using was an hour's drive from our house. Every day during the IVF process we'd get up at 4:00, hit the road by 4:30, arrive at 5:30 for the various procedures, the ultrasounds, and all. Then we'd drive all the way back so I could be at work by 8:00. Needless to say, this was really stressful for both of us.

The first cycle seemed to go well. Mary developed lots of mature follicles—so many that her stomach was tender—but we didn't end up pregnant. We were devastated. On top of it all, lots of our friends started to get pregnant and would avoid Mary, which was really painful for her. She felt really left out of this new "club." Then, as our friends started having their kids, they got busy, and we saw them less and less. Everything was shifting and changing for everyone else, but we felt really, really stuck. And with fewer and fewer friends, to boot! It got to the point where the only friends we invited over to our house were the ones who were also child free.

We also avoided everything baby related. The worst was getting a baby shower invitation. Mary would torture herself over whether to go or not to go. Of course, we had to buy a gift. Sometimes she'd decide to go but then couldn't even get in the car to make the drive, she'd be so upset. Or she'd drive all the way there and then just park a few houses away and just watch. It was horrible.

We would avoid baby clothes in stores, doing whatever it took— even walking a mile around—just not to have to walk through the baby department. We'd eat only at more expensive restaurants because they usually didn't have a lot of kids there. Our sex life completely collapsed. It was no longer fun. The only reason we ever even had sex was to make a baby. By this time we weren't feeling much of anything except anguish. The sex brought no pleasure or closeness. There's nothing like fear of failure to break the mood.

By our count, Mary had sixty-two periods during the time we tried to get pregnant. That's sixty-two months—more than five years—of feeling like total failures.

We tried everything, even listened to some old wives' tales about not wearing briefs, because they'd lower your sperm count. Even though my sperm count was never an issue. In fact, at one point the

*clinic even approached me about being a donor for another couple.
Whew. That was a big thorn to Mary, who took it as a slam on her,
like she was "the problem." (I declined.)*

*Mary went to great lengths to take her mind off our fertility
problems. She enrolled in cooking school and became an amazing
chef. Once, Wolfgang Puck even called our house to ask Mary to
come and make pastries for his Academy Award parties. She declined. She was just too depressed and defeated.*

*But that didn't stop her from enrolling in college and becoming
the first member of her family to get a degree! She even went on and
became a CPA, passing the test on the first try. She also re-did our
home. We got a few side benefits out of this, for sure, but we still
weren't getting pregnant.*

*Finally, after all those years, she was diagnosed with "nonspe-
cific" infertility. We were told it was an immunological issue for
which there was no good treatment, just experimental stuff. It was
so excruciating for both of us that nothing was technically "wrong"
with either of us but we still couldn't make a baby. Someone at the
clinic said to Mary that her uterus was like a "lion's den" to an embryo, meaning a hostile environment. What a terrible thing to say to
someone in such distress!*

*The specialist told us we'd probably never succeed on our own.
Well, at least that gave us a bit of closure, but we were left with lots
of questions, starting with what to do with our frozen embryos.*

*Not ones to give up easily, we did try an experimental immuniza-
tion treatment that involved injecting my blood into Mary's skin to
see if she was reacting to my DNA. Yep, that was it. As soon as they
did the injection she felt this searing pain and a severe skin reaction.
We even hung in through a few more cycles, just to be absolutely sure,
but with no success.*

Finally, we accepted the reality that the only way we would have a baby would be through adoption, and twice we thought we had a deal, but then ended up getting ripped off by the birth mothers. On the third attempt, we did get our baby, only to have the mother change her mind and take her back. It was almost impossible not to feel just totally victimized by life at this point. We were both devastated and completely at the breaking point.

We started making arrangements to adopt a baby from China, and eighteen months later we brought home our beautiful daughter Laney. As we adjusted to life with our baby, we decided to try again. We did some immunization treatments so that Mary's body would be less likely to reject the embryos created with my sperm, and all that took time. But, unbelievably, she got pregnant. Maybe the tides were turning?

We both spent her entire pregnancy riddled with fear. When we found out she was carrying twins, I got really scared, but Mary was overjoyed. Then she started spotting. We had lost one of the babies. Mary went into mourning. Frankly at that point I didn't know what to feel. And then Justine arrived. Healthy. Beautiful beyond words. But by then our marriage was shattered.

The whole process changed us both. Our world became all about the kids. I started calling in sick to work a lot and just started living on the fantasy that the money would "just come." Of course, I was eventually laid off, and we had to file for bankruptcy to prevent the loss of our house and get out from under the growing mountain of debt. But even that didn't help. We lost the house anyway. No one will let you keep a house when you can't pay the mortgage. And we ended up divorcing.

We have two great kids, Laney, adopted from China, and Justine. I see them weekly, but I lost my marriage in the process and miss so much of the kids' lives by not seeing them every day. I see now that I made so many mistakes, and some days I wish I could do everything over. Through this experience, I have come to believe a few things about men and women and family:

Women tend to get at least some feeling of their value as individuals from having a family. This becomes stronger when the choice to have a baby is "taken away." It is extremely strong in those women who pursue their hopes of starting a family and endure the ordeal of infertility.

Men tend to get at least some feeling of their value as individuals from being able to provide for a family. It is not as devastating for men if the choice of having a family is taken away. But it is devastating to see the one you love in such pain when you are totally helpless to do anything about it.

Going into infertility, neither men nor women have any idea what is going to hit them. Women do have the focal point of a baby to hold on to against the obstacles. Men do not have this focus and must roll with the punches.

Men don't understand what women are going through, at least not until after they are through it.

During their ordeal, James couldn't really allow himself to feel his true feelings. It was only afterward that he connected with himself, and by then his primary feeling was grief. He is adamant that he would never say "If I had it to do over, I wouldn't," but he clearly wishes things had been very different.

There's no question that men and women experience infertility differently. But it's important to remember that men have an emotional response to infertility, too. So ladies, cut your partner some slack. I know it's hard to do that when you're going through something so emotional and devastating yourself. And no one says you have to be a saint about it. But do try to give your partner some space to express himself and share his feelings. If asking him outright doesn't work, maybe just acknowledging the fact that he has feelings and being sensitive to them will be enough. Above all, try to keep the lines of communication open so that he feels able to be honest about what he's going through. And if he *is* shut down, it may be time for some counseling.

Resources

Even if you've never considered counseling, now might be the time to start. The best way to find a good counselor is by personal recommendation. Ask a friend, relative, clergyperson, your doctor, or a trusted colleague for names of counselors or therapists they like and trust, or ask your fertility specialist if she or he knows of any local support groups for men in your situation. You deserve to have a place to talk about what's going on for you, as a man, where you won't feel judged or like you have to walk on eggshells.

CHAPTER 10

Hang In There!

Guy and I had a happy ending to our infertility story. And so can you. The funny thing about the end of most infertility stories, whether they lead to in vitro fertilization (IVF), gamete intra-fallopian transfer (GIFT), surrogacy, or adoption, is that they also mark the beginning of a whole new adventure: as a parent, with a family, a dream come true.

For Guy and me, parenthood is a more loving and rewarding and incredible experience than we could have ever imagined. Our infertility journey had a miraculous ending. Nicholas, Sierra, and Sabrina are the joys of our life. It's hard to picture my life, our lives, before they were here. Oh sure, I remember a time when life was all about me. That was nice, and I remember it fondly. But the joys of *that* life pale in comparison to the rewards of parenting these three amazing creatures. I am richer and more fulfilled than I have been from anything else I've ever done in my life.

People often look at Guy and me and think we have the perfect life. Money, celebrity, three beautiful children, our health, each other. But our lives aren't perfect. Far from it, actually. We deal with all the same things everyone else does. We have the same choices to make, the same opportunities and decisions. The same hardships and failures, rewards and celebrations. It truly is no different. Oh, I'll be the first to admit that my life is very rich and that I have had many blessings. But as you quickly discover once you become a parent, it's not the things in your life that fill the empty spaces in your heart.

As our children grow, Guy and I will undoubtedly face more troubled times. That's just the nature of raising kids. Being a good parent, being the kind of parent you want to be, making good choices, seeing your children through difficult moments and feelings and sometimes through serious challenges to their health and well-being—none of this is easy. Wonderful, amazing, incredible? Yes. As well as exhausting, challenging, and just plain hard work.

It's was a real shock to find out we couldn't have children the old-fashioned way. Like you, we were shaken out of that state of blissful ignorance, that smug confidence that we would get pregnant readily. We had to live with the exceedingly frustrating diagnosis of unexplainable infertility, first coping with the routines of some relatively inexpensive and uncomplicated fertility treatments and then, after many months of devastating disappointments, stepping up to some of the most high-tech interventions available today. We had the experience of birthing our own children and also of bringing in a surrogate—and along the way, we met so many other women and men struggling to create and build their families, just like us. Many of them were pretty freaked out to find themselves having so much trouble. Some of them were really scared, and a great many of them felt all too alone.

No question about it, a diagnosis of infertility can knock you right on your butt; the process is an emotional, physical, and financial roller coaster that you fear you'll never be able to get off. I'm here to tell you, it's not fun to be on an examination table with your feet in the stirrups with two doctors, three nurses, and a medical student staring up your vagina. But as embarrassing as that may be, as uncomfortable as you can even imagine those circumstances to be, that's your new reality. You might as well get used to it. Might as well rewrite those baby dreams, too. Because there will be no wonderful night of love in the privacy of your own bedroom to look back on. No memory of warm summer breezes, a romantic dinner, or too many sips of champagne. Our baby-making memories won't be the same as everyone else's, but that doesn't mean they can't be sweet. And trust me, it's worth going through whatever it takes.

If you're just starting down the infertility road, you're going to find that you have to put your trust into your partner in a way you never would have anticipated, never even thought possible. He or she may become your chemist, mixing potions and cures, then injecting them into your body with the skill and confidence you could—*should*—have to expect only out of professionally trained medical personnel. He or she may become your taskmaster, reminding you to take your temperature first thing in the morning before you've even moved a muscle let alone had your first cup of coffee, taking you to your appointments, seeing you through some of the darkest, most primal feelings that come with the territory of infertility. You must allow the experience to strengthen your bond with your mate or you'll sink. Stay united in your goal to have a family. Do whatever it takes to get there.

And keep this in mind: One day the memory of pulling your husband into the women's room of a crowded restaurant so he can shoot you full of fertility drugs that make you feel like a lunatic will make you laugh. It really will.

Let's Share Our Stories— and Our Strength

Promise me you will challenge your own feelings of shame and try to speak openly and honestly about your situation. Continued reluctance to speak about infertility or even to share the problem with close family and friends, as I've said so many times in this book, only reinforces the isolation and shame, further cutting you off from support and resources at a time when you need them the most. How many times I saw that shame on the faces of the women and couples I met! It makes me want to scream.

The taboo surrounding infertility is astounding. Mind-boggling. Almost incomprehensible when you think of all the other kinds of information people so readily share in whatever forum they find themselves in. We need to change that. We need to make information more accessible. We need to talk to each other and to the world about how devastating and debilitating infertility can be, both emotionally and financially, and also share our reasons to be hopeful and stay strong.

In 2005, the cable channel VH1 aired a special about our infertility struggle. They called it *Cindy Margolis Inside/Out*. I was never so proud. Sure, it was hard to have cameras around 24/7, and I had many doubts and misgivings about the decision to allow this televised glimpse into our personal life. Especially after they ended up filming one of our very saddest and unsuccessful in vitro attempts. But when I witnessed how profoundly it affected people and saw the awareness it created, I felt sure there was nothing more positive and useful I could have done to help other couples who are trying without success to have a baby. E-mails from women and struggling couples poured into my website. Thousands and thousands of letters each month told me that this kind of exposure, this kind of truth telling, is exactly what's needed.

I hope that after reading this book, you will never again feel that you have nowhere to turn to find the information and resources you need, the support and guidance you deserve. I hope you realize that you are far, far from alone.

Find people with whom you can share your fears and joys along the infertility journey. Please do whatever it takes not to feel embarrassed or ashamed to admit that you need help. Statistics now tell us that one in every five women and couples is having trouble conceiving. That's a lot of us!

The reasons for this are as varied and complicated as infertility itself, but such huge numbers should surely convince us of one thing: There's nothing to be ashamed of. You are in very good company. Chances are, in fact, that someone very close to you is experiencing infertility, too. Find that person and start talking. Share your fears and your hopes and your resources.

There's certainly reason for hope. New legislation is being proposed all the time to protect or help infertile couples; insurance carriers are wising up and picking up the banner. There are many new treatments coming our way, less invasive treatments that require fewer drugs and carry lower price tags. And new voices are continually joining our chorus in support of opening the physical, emotional, and financial doors for couples undergoing infertility.

My dream for each one of you reading this book is that by now you will:

- Know that you are not alone.

- Be inspired to continue on your journey to create or expand your family.

- Have taken my message to heart: For everyone with a dream of having a family, there *is* a way.

Please, never give up the faith. Hold to your dream of becoming a parent. It may take a little longer than you'd hoped, it may happen in a way you could never have imagined, it may test you and stretch you farther than you thought you could be stretched, but if you stay strong, I can promise you, you will find a way. And it'll all be worth it.

The moment you hold your beautiful baby in your arms, you will forget the past and move with astounding love into the future, becoming a parent at last. However you do it, however you come to be a parent, you will have participated in the great miracle that is life. As Guy likes to say, once you become a family, you pretty quickly forget how you did it. And that's a fact. You have my word.

Love, Cindy *XO*

GLOSSARY

Assisted hatching: a micro-manipulation procedure in which a small opening is made in the zona pellucida, the shell surrounding the embryo, to maximize implantation.

Assisted reproductive therapy (ART): technologically advanced procedure used to improve fertility by assisting fertilization of the egg by the sperm and maximizing the chances of embryo implantation.

Blastocyst: an embryo on its fifth or sixth day of life, immediately before implantation in the uterus.

Embryo: the earliest stages of the development of a fertilized egg. It is the embryo that is implanted into the uterus during in vitro fertilization.

Embryo banking: storing embryos for future use. Sometimes they are frozen, or cryo-preserved, for purposes of delaying fertility or to allow for future use of excess embryos created during an in vitro fertilization cycle for later use.

Endometriosis: a disease in which tissue that normally lines the uterus is found in other parts of the body, usually in the pelvic cavity, where it can hinder the function of the fallopian tubes and thereby cause infertility. Some patients with endometriosis suffer great pain during their periods or throughout the month.

Fetus: the very young baby, after the embryo stage and before delivery.

Gamete: the sperm or egg.

Gamete intrafallopian transfer (GIFT): a procedure whereby gametes (both eggs and sperm) are placed into the fallopian tubes(s) laparoscopically to assist with conception.

Gonadotropin-releasing hormone (GnRH) agonists/antagonists: medications used to prevent premature ovulation in assisted reproductive technology cycles. One brand name is Lupron.

Hyperstimulation: overstimulation of the ovaries as a result of assisted reproduction, causing everything from enlargement of the ovaries and fluid retention around the abdomen to nausea, vomiting, and shortness of breath to a life-threatening buildup of fluids around the body organs (heart, lungs, kidneys), and a drop in blood fluid content. If you experience any of these symptoms after an in vitro fertilization procedure, call your doctor immediately or, if symptoms are severe, call 911 or go to an emergency room. This condition requires urgent medical care and hospitalization to prevent liver failure, stroke, or heart damage.

Hysterosalpingography (HSG): a procedure in which dye is injected into the uterus, which is then X-rayed continuously as the dye travels up into the fallopian tubes to determine if they are blocked in any way.

Intracytoplasmic sperm injection (ICSI): sperm is injected into the egg to assist in fertilization. Can assist with male factor and some immunological causes of infertility.

Intrauterine insemination (IUI): a clinical procedure in which fresh or frozen sperm are isolated from other components of the semen by washing, tested for motility, then (if motile) placed directly into a woman's uterus using a soft catheter. Often the first prescribed treatment. Can be used with or without fertility drugs.

In vitro fertilization (IVF): a procedure involving removing a woman's eggs from her uterus, collecting a man's sperm, and introducing eggs and sperm in a Petri dish to optimize chances of fertilization. The resulting embryos are then implanted in a woman; often a normal pregnancy ensues. Increases your chances of multiple births.

Laparoscopy or laparoscopic surgery: a minimally invasive surgery is performed with the aid of a tiny camera (about the size of a fountain pen). One tiny incision is made through which the scope is inserted, and then another tiny incision or two is made for the surgical instruments. Such procedures minimize pain, scarring, and recovery time.

Long protocol: an in vitro fertilization–stimulation protocol using a gonadotropin-releasing hormone agonist (for example, Lupron), beginning approximately one week after ovulation.

Polycystic ovarian syndrome (PCOS): a condition that results in poor egg quality because the follicles never fully mature. The most common symptoms of PCOS, other than trouble getting pregnant, are increased hair growth, irregular periods, and unusual weight gain, even when you're dieting and exercising. PCOS not only can cause infertility but can also increase your risk of diabetes and cardiovascular disease later in life. It is a fairly common syndrome, affecting approximately 10 percent of women worldwide.

Preimplantation genetic diagnosis (PGD): the evaluation of the chromosomes of an early embryo.

Zygote intrafallopian transfer (ZIFT): a laparoscopic procedure in which zygotes are placed into the fallopian tube(s) to assist with conception.

Zygote: a fertilized egg; the pre-embryo stage occurring one day after egg retrieval.

RESOURCES

Below are some of the resources I found useful as I searched for credible and up-to-date information on infertility and treatment options. This list is by no means exhaustive, but I hope you'll find it useful as you begin your own search for information.

In Vitro Fertilization/Infertility Services

RESOLVE: The National Infertility Association
7910 Woodmont Avenue
Suite 1350
Bethesda, MD 20814
301-652-8585; 888-623-0744 (help line)
www.resolve.org

The InterNational Council on Infertility Information Dissemination
P.O. Box 6836
Arlington, VA 22206
703-379-9178
www.inciid.org

The Endometriosis Association
8585 North Seventy-sixth Place
Milwaukee, WI 53223
414-355-2200
www.endometriosisassn.org

Polycystic Ovarian Syndrome Association
P.O. Box 3403
Englewood, CO 80111
www.PCOSupport.org

Internet Health Resources
www.ihr.com/infertility

Society for Assisted Reproductive Technology
205-978-5000
www.sart.org/find_frm.html

The American Fertility Association
888-917-3777
www.theafa.org

Fertility Plus
www.fertilityplus.com

Conceptual Options
12780 Danielson Court
Suite B
Poway, CA 92064
858-748-4222
www.conceptualoptions.com

Male Infertility

The Men's Room
www.inciid.org/forums/mens_room/index.html

Surrogacy

Surrogate Moms Online
www.surromomsonline.com

Adoption & Assisted Reproduction Law Offices of Diane Michelsen
Family Formation
3190 Old Tunnel Road
Lafayette, CA 94549
925-945-1880
www.familyformation.com

Everything Surrogacy
www.everythingssurrogacy.com

All About Surrogacy
www.allaboutsurrogacy.com

Center for Surrogate Parenting, Inc.
West Coast Office
15821 Ventura Boulevard
Suite 675
Encino, CA 91346
818-788-8288
East Coast Office
9 State Circle
Suite 302
Annapolis, MD 21401
410-990-9860
www.creatingfamilies.com

Fertility Plus
www.fertilityplus.com

Sperm Bank Directory
www.spermbankdirectory.com

Egg Donation, Inc.
15821 Ventura Boulevard
Suite 675
Encino, CA 91436
818-385-0950
www.eggdonor.com

Choice Moms
www.choosingsinglemotherhood.com

National Association of Single Mothers
www.singlemothers.org

Erickson Law
Theresa Erickson, Esq.
12780 Danielson Court
Suite B
Poway, CA 92064
866-757-4994
www.ericksonlaw.net

Adoption

National Adoption Center
1500 Walnut Street
Suite 701
Philadelphia, PA 19102
800-TO-ADOPT
www.adopt.org

American Adoptions
National Offices
9101 West 110th Street
Second floor, Suite 200
Overland Park, KS 66210
800-ADOPTION
www.americanadoptions.com

Children's Hope International
11780 Borman Drive
St. Louis, MO 63146
314-890-0086
www.childrenshopeint.org

The Human Rights Campaign
www.hrc.org

The North American Council on Adoptable Children
970 Raymond Avenue
Suite 106
St. Paul, MN 55114
651-644-3036
www.nacac.org

Commonwealth Adoptions International
877-311-4646
www.commonwealthadoption.org

INDEX

ABOUT THE AUTHORS

Photo by Andy Pearlman

The most popular celebrity on the Internet, **Cindy Margolis** is a supermodel and an accomplished host, producer, and actress.

While best known for her number-one-rated celebrity website, "The Most Downloaded Woman" has been labeled a phenomenon by everyone from Yahoo!, America Online's Woman of the Year, and *Guinness Book of World Records* to *Forbes*, *Time*, and *People* Magazine's "50 Most Beautiful People."

Born and raised in the San Fernando Valley by her single mother, Cindy first took the Internet world by storm with her innovative fan-friendly website that offered everything from girlfriend and motherly advice to e-commerce and live streaming video. Her "Girl Talk" section is one of the most popular communities on the Internet.

Near and dear to her heart, Cindy is the Official Celebrity Spokesperson for RESOLVE: The National Infertility Association. Cindy serves as a voice for women and men struggling with infertility to help raise awareness about the issues and to support people experiencing infertility, from lobbying for greater insurance coverage, research, and public education to helping more women and men cope with their challenge and make informed choices about their treatment and other options. Cindy travels the country to tell the story of her struggle through tragedy to triumph in having her precious baby boy and her journey with surrogacy to have her beautiful twin girls.

Courtesy of the author

Kathy Kanable is an accomplished writer and entrepreneur. As director of Internet Operations for Cindy Margolis, Inc., Kathy maintains www.cindymargolis.com, one of the top-rated celebrity websites in the world.

Kathy has worked as a passionate activist for government reform, serving three terms and two County Executives in her home state of Michigan. A married mother of two, she currently resides in Arizona with her husband, Tom.

Photo by Niki Fine

Dr. Snunit Ben-Ozer is board-certified in both Reproductive Endocrinology and Infertility (REI) and Obstetrics and Gynecology and is an Assistant Clinical Professor at UCLA and the founder of the Tree of Life Center in Encino and Beverly Hills, CA.

Her training is buttressed by more than eleven years of clinical expertise in Assisted Reproductive Technologies (ART), ovulation induction, and surgery. Thus, she can uniquely utilize the full therapeutic continuum for her patients. Her nationally ranked pregnancy rates with IVF, GIFT, and ZIFT, and success with less technologically challenging treatment options, reflect her expertise and compassion. Dr. Ben-Ozer has made numerous national media appearances, and has lectured widely on the subject of infertility.